a

The Lure of the Lake District

THE LURE OF THE LAKE DISTRICT

PLACES, PEOPLE AND PASSIONS

Steve Goodier

FRANCES LINCOLN LIMITED

PUBLISHERS

I WOULD LIKE TO DEDICATE THIS BOOK TO MY WIFE
PAULA AND CHILDREN DANIELLE AND LUKE – WHO
SHARED THE ADVENTURES

A SPECIAL THANKS TO TERRY FLETCHER AND KEVIN
HOPKINSON OF CUMBRIA MAGAZINE WHERE SOME OF
THE IDEAS IN THIS BOOK WERE FIRST PUBLISHED

Frances Lincoln Limited
4 Torriano Mews
Torriano Avenue
London NW5 2RZ

The Lure of the Lake District
Copyright © 2010 Frances Lincoln Limited

A catalogue record for this book is available from the British Library

ISBN: 978-0-7112-3169-6

Printed in China

9 8 7 6 5 4 3 2 1

Contents

I.

A LOVE OF THE LAKES

The English Lake District means many different things to many different people, but for walkers, climbers and outdoor lovers generally it has to be the mecca, the Holy Grail of the home nations' mountain world. Many may point at Scotland – Fort William, nestling beneath Ben Nevis, is vying to become the self styled 'outdoor capital of the United Kingdom', but for me, and I suspect thousands of others, the towns of Keswick and Ambleside have to be considered as serious contenders for this unofficial crown. And Lakeland as a whole must rank in the top one or two of the premier league of mountain sports locations as the spell it casts over people is hard to break.

The lure of the lakes takes many forms and is an addiction that has no obvious and instant remedy. I have walked and climbed in many parts of the world and all over England, Ireland, Wales and Scotland and yet, after almost a quarter of a century of climbing these magnificent fells, I still return here often and yearn for their pleasures when I am away.

I have often sat quietly and tried to put a finger on just what this magnetic draw is and usually failed as we are not looking at one specific and isolated facet of this fascinating landscape but at a combination, a kaleidoscope of many different segments that can interchange and switch places as time changes and passes and seasons come and go. Even the weather has an influence on these phenomena and to complicate it even more, it is something we tailor to ourselves and it therefore becomes an individual experience moulded by our years of exploring. And again, because there is so much variety, we are constantly revising our current favourite memory, place, mountain or experience.

With so many variables it is no wonder we can't define just what this lure of Lakeland constitutes but we continue to try, albeit subconsciously most of the time. But mostly we just keep coming back to partake of the endless and free pleasure this outdoor wonderland gives unselfishly to us.

The decades pass and although the infrastructure may change and evolve and our 'hundred-mile-an-hour world' encroaches ever more into this sanctuary, the backdrop; the stage against which we enact our dramas hardly alters at all.

The mountains and the lakes that combine to give the Lake District its uniqueness are the same today as they were in the days of William Wordsworth or when Alfred Wainwright first conceived the idea of his *Pictorial Guides*. True, paths change but usually not by much; routes become wider as erosion takes its toll – an unfortunate side effect of the popularity this area has – but if you placed a map of the summits, lakes and paths from 100 years ago over a Harvey's or Ordnance Survey Map of today, the differences would be minimal.

The lure of the lakes is also the lure of the mountains, the two being intertwined and inseparable. Although we call the region 'The Lake District' it is those wonderful fells that are the big attraction here.

Fell walking, peak bagging, gully climbing, rock climbing, scrambling and valley walking all form part of this pastime. I am loathe to call it a sport as this bears little resemblance (or shouldn't) to the wonderful attractions of packing a rucksack and heading for the heights. However, more and more the competitive nature of the early twenty first century is creeping into our hill days with people pushing for faster rounds, more mountains in set times, younger ages for bagging all the tops and setting off to beat everyone else to

the top and be back at the car before a set time to give time for...
well, to give time for whatever could be better than being up high
in Lakeland! These aspects of our nature have no place on the fells
but it's not really our fault, we are products of our time and our time
promotes speed and extra fast living.

However, this is not the place for looking at the negative aspects
of our chosen arena. Suffice to say that it is with us, the fell walkers
and climbers, that the answer to this ephemeral madness lies. We
can choose to slow down and take the fells as they should be taken,
or we can choose the other path and leave ourselves wondering why
we no longer get the fulfilment we used to from our fell days.

Throughout this book you will find a thread that connects the
chapters. That is an appreciation of the utter magic of this region
that has enslaved me for a quarter of a century and will do so, I
guess, until the day they scatter my ashes high on one of these
wonderful mountain tops.

And I make no apologies for the fact that the bias of these pages
is towards the high places, the tops and ridges, that combine and
form the backdrop to the 'shining levels' of the lakes to give us such
a unique landscape.

You will find much in these pages that relates to my own
experiences and memories of the Lakeland and much of the folklore
and history that I find so bewitching too. I hope I will impart to
you the feeling I get as I drop, for instance, from Thelkeld on the
A66 towards the Vale of Keswick and the north western fells open
before me as I drive, or of the joy I feel driving along Haweswater
towards Mardale Head on a late winter's early morning with snow
on the tops and a full day of winter fell walking ahead of me in good
company. I could go on and on with the examples, such is my love
of the area but if I do no more than make you reminisce about your
own days in Lakeland, I feel I will have achieved my goal. If I make

you go out and relive them again, so much the better.

The Lakes are for the young and the old. The young can plan and do, the old can remember and recollect.

Lakeland is timeless and impossible to define in one book or maybe not even in a hundred. And in the pages that follow I have added my own small testimony to the legacy of literature that has gone before.

And as the emphasis of what follows is on the high places then maybe we ought to begin with a brief look at the birth of fell walking as a pastime. The origins of the rock climbing fraternity are well documented but a lot of people assume that people have always walked the fells and that there was never an evolution that took place and led people from the valleys and onto the seemingly out of reach tops. But there was and there were two distinct people who led this revolution and I feel at the very start of these pages it would be a good place to set the scene and outline how it all began and where our roots as true Lakeland fell lovers really lie.

THE FIRST FELL WALKERS

Not so long ago I found myself descending the top rocks of Causey Pike on a warm October afternoon with the Vale of Keswick laid out below me and not another soul in sight. It felt like I was the only fell walker in not just the Lake District, but possibly the whole north of England. To me this felt like it must have for the very first hardy soul who ventured onto our Lakeland hills all those years ago – empty tops, acres of space and the world at their feet. True, there wouldn't have been the wide path – but such things are a direct descendent of their initial endeavours.

My mind began to wander. I had just completed the Coledale Horseshoe in what I felt was a very respectable time and I knew that the first recorded person to have done this round was that energetic

Lakeland poet Samuel Taylor Coleridge in September 1800. But even he wasn't the very first to be attracted to the high places, although to read his descriptions of his exploits, especially his epic descent of Broad Stand on Scafell on 5th August 1802, you would think he was the founder member of The Ramblers Association!

Coleridge liked nothing better than to tramp the tops; he recorded ascents of Carrock Fell, Bowscale Fell and Bannerdale Crags. He also walked by moonlight along the Helvellyn Ridge and his close friend William Wordsworth was noted for his long distance fell walking exploits.

However, we have to go back a bit further than these two to find someone we could really consider to be the first true fell walker. It would be fair to say that the shepherds had wandered the heights for centuries as part of their daily work, but none had recorded their trips and none considered it unusual.

The birth of fell walking was directly connected to the explosion of tourism that brought the wealthy to the Lakes in their hundreds in the late eighteenth and early nineteenth centuries. We often think it must have been a lot longer ago than that; but in reality, less than 250 years back in time, Lakeland was a remote outpost in northern England with poor road networks.

All that began to change when the likes of Thomas Pennant, the Jesuit Father Thomas West and the Reverend William Gilpin began to explore the area and record their wanderings in books and travel guides to the region. Of the three, it was West who really got things going. Author of the classic *The Antiquities of Furness* he gave selected viewpoints where his readers could use a 'Claude Glass' to see the most breathtaking spectacles. Inspired by these three, more books appeared and the roads improved to accommodate the extra visitors.

However, none of these early writers ventured into the high places and climbed the fells. They were still considered too dangerous and out of the reach of the ordinary tourist. The likes of Gilpin, West and Pennant drove or rode on their explorations, and when a horse or carriage could go no further they simply gave it up and covered their omissions with excuses of impassable dale heads where only shepherds could go and then for only a few weeks each year. Sty Head, for instance, was listed in this category for many years and later, when it became obvious it was passable year round, it was left unexplored because it was considered the sort of place outlaws took refuge and therefore much too dangerous to venture into.

But things were getting better, the visitors more adventurous and the tourist industry was beginning to get into gear. Many looked to the fell tops and wondered what it would be like to go up and explore them but most dismissed it as beyond their capabilities.

Guides began to appear at the best hotels in Windermere, Ambleside and Keswick to exploit this omission, but mostly they offered low level walks and boat trips along the lakes. The one exception was the ascent of Skiddaw which could be achieved on a pony and was considered safe enough even for women. Some of the more forward thinking guides offered guiding up Helvellyn from the west (Thirlspot or Wythburn) but it was considered a dodgy practice.

And then along came an ex-army captain by the name of Joseph Budworth. In him we find what we really must consider as the first fell walker, or at least the first we can see who went into print. Budworth was born in 1756 and died in 1825 and spent his early adult life as soldier leaving military service with the rank of Captain. He married a rich Irish woman called Elizabeth Palmer and inherited large estates in Ireland. Now independently wealthy and free from work, he set about living the rest of his life in seclusion and regularly travelled and wrote about his exploits.

He visited the lakes aged thirty nine in 1795 and afterwards wrote his best known work on the trip *A Fortnight's Ramble to the Lakes*.

It would be true to say that two years earlier than this there was a recorded ascent of Blencathra up Scales Fell led by a Threlkeld man called Mr Clement, but this was a 'one off' and undertaken as an alternative to the crowds who now rode ponies up Skiddaw.

It was Captain Joseph Budworth who epitomises what we would recognise today as the typical and determined fell walker. You may find him referred to, or writing under the name of, Joseph Palmer, a surname he adopted in honour of his marriage to Elizabeth and to be fair, it would be a small price for any of us to pay if we found ourselves suddenly able to follow our dreams without any financial constraint.

Budworth was the stereotype for the modern fell walker. He thought nothing of huge distances, cared little about the weather and considered getting soaked to the skin as part of the game. He was always willing to detour to take in extra summits and generally climbed mountains because they were there and he liked doing it. He was full of energy and never passed up the chance for a hill walk. In his original fortnight's break in the Lakes he covered 240 miles, a respectable distance when you consider that few, if any, of the fells would have had paths on them.

He made the first recorded ascent of Helm Crag and, on a circular tour from Ambleside to Coniston via Hawkeshead was persuaded by a local farmer to detour and have a go at climbing Coniston Old Man – or as Budworth quaintly puts it, "symptoms appeared of wishing to ascend it" – I like that!

Budworth made great use of the Ambleside guide Robin Partridge who worked out of the town's Salutation Hotel, and it was with him that he undertook the adventurous (at least for those days) ascent of Helvellyn. This is the first recorded ascent of the mountain you will come across and in true 'alpine spirit', he and Partridge left Ambleside at four in the morning. He also threw in Fairfield, Dollywaggon Pike and Nethermost Pike to just to make it a longer day – does he remind you of yourself a bit? I can certainly see similarities to my walking days, and companions who have tramped after me on one of my 'we might as well include such and such in the day's tally before we go down' excursions would nod in agreement!

He cared little for food (but was very fond of huge meals before or after a day on the tops) and was grateful for whatever he could get at the time when on the fells. He liked to carry brandy on his walks and was always insatiably thirsty, drinking long from mountain streams.

If it began with Joseph Budworth, the gauntlet was picked up in admirable style by one Edward Baines little more than thirty years later. Like many others who came to the Lakes at this time, he wrote a book (a very good one) called *A Companion to the Lakes* and it was he who dispensed with the use of guides and made ascents on his own or with companions. It is a natural evolution that took place in the Alps and other mountain areas, one just doesn't think of it happening in Lakeland. But with the arrival of Baines, the work of the guides began to come to an end. He was a pioneering spirit and made the first recorded ascent of Striding Edge on Helvellyn. Apart from using an occasional farmer to help him in difficult terrain, he dispensed with professional guiding altogether. His tally was impressive and, like Budworth before him, he loved 'multi summit' days. His list of early ascents included Bowfell and Scafell Pike and he loved wandering through passes and over summits linking valleys and towns. He spent a lot of his spare time holidaying in the Lakes and it would be true to say he opened up the high places to the ordinary man in a way that had not been achieved before.

And from there things just kept developing and the tracks began to appear up familiar routes and, one by one, the remaining summits were 'bagged' by the early adventurers.

It's sobering to think that what we practice each weekend is barely over two hundred years old and that the thousands who tramp the Lakes fells nowadays were preceded by a mere one or two. We must assume that Coleridge and Wordsworth were inspired by our two heroes and we have to concede that we owe a great debt to these two men whom you've probably never heard of before.

So the next time you reach a summit cairn drink a silent toast to Joseph Budworth and Edward Baines – for between them they founded the modern pastime of Lakeland fell walking. And what a legacy they left us in their wake. When you try to analyse fell walking and mountain or rock climbing, it is soon apparent that it defies ordinary logic in its basic simplicity. It costs very little to spend a day on the fells or the crags and yet the rewards it bestows on its devotees are far in excess of the tiny bit of expenditure called for. You drive to your chosen car park, don your boots and rucksack and well...the outdoor world of Lakeland is quite simply at your feet.

It seems almost criminal to get so much for so little especially in our consumer dominated world where money shelled out is believed to be in direct balance to satisfaction received in return. And yet, for me and many others down the years, these Lake District days have been the highlights of my weeks and the focus of my dreams when I have been absent. The changing seasons and the constantly fluctuating weather, the light on the fells, the many and varied fell tops themselves, these have all combined to cast this magic spell over me. But I suppose above all it has to be the seasons, the times of the year, that have given me so much variety and which come back to me so vividly when I close my eyes and dream of the Lakes.

Each season has its own magic and special memories for each individual. For me, it's winter on the Coniston Fells with ice hard on the paths and the smoke from the village below rising into a still winter's dusk as we pad down carefully by head torch light at day's end. Or spring in Borrowdale with that feeling that only May gives as you sit by Derwentwater on Friday evening knowing that the weekend in front of you has a good forecast and you are a 'freeman' of the hills for the next forty eight hours at least.

Summer can sometimes be a disappointment with low cloud and greyer days bringing drizzle, but when we do chance upon a good day what can beat setting off at first light for an early morning round of Fairfield and being on your way down for a breakfast in Ambleside as the majority of the day's walkers are just on their way up? Or leaving Glenridding shortly after midnight on mid-summer's day to climb up Kepple Cove to watch the sun rise on Helvellyn on the longest day of the year with the many others who will have gathered there? Autumn can mean days on the fells above Ullswater with the lake steely grey and still and the trees around Pooley Bridge an endless variety of reds and yellows. Each season has its own magic and special memories for each individual, but let's just take the time to look at a few of those times and perhaps take a different slant on them than you may have considered before.

Winter – A Different Way to Spend Christmas and New Year

Many years ago, long before we had kids and Christmas Day became a major family event, we used to forsake our turkey and mince pies on 25 December and head out to the Lakeland fells. I know it's probably not everyone's cup of tea, but we had some really memorable days. For several years we had met up with friends on Boxing Day for a walk over Blencathra or the Langdale Pikes and one year someone suggested we give it a try on Christmas Day.

The fells are often busy on Boxing Day so it seemed likely they might be quiet on the main day of the Christmas festivities. Our first venture was to be Helvellyn and we hoped for full winter conditions but it looked unlikely as December ticked by and the weather stayed foggy, grey and damp. However, a week before Christmas, a cold front dropped down through Scotland bringing snow to the Lakes. It didn't last long low down but the tops were covered and each night saw clear skies and plummeting temperatures. Perfect conditions for a winter traverse of Striding Edge and Swirral Edge.

Five of us met at the car park in Glenridding early on Christmas morning and the world seemed as empty as the parking area. Odd lights were on in houses, smoke trickled from chimneys into the clear morning air and we set off feeling very smug. The forecast was excellent and we anticipated a decent mountaineering route and a summit all to ourselves.

Our first 'meet' set the tone for all those that followed. Being Christmas anyway it's a great time to get together with friends you haven't seen for some time; our group lived in various parts of the country and we only really got to meet up a few times a year – throwing in an unusual fell walk was just the icing on the seasonal cake! To make it special we imposed an element of silliness. To take part you had to don a red Father Christmas hat and carry mince pies, turkey butties and Christmas cake in the rucksack. Tinsel around the rucksack was optional but nearly always included, as was some form of alcoholic beverage. So, looking like something out of a pantomime, we took our time working our way up to the hole in the wall and the start of Striding Edge constantly scratching our heads which were maddeningly itchy due to the nylon Santa head gear!

Striding Edge did not disappoint and it was a full crampons and ice axe job all the way to the final bad step and then up to the summit of Helvellyn. The air stayed crystal clear all day and the temperature below freezing – it was one of those rare winter days that you always remember. Tramping along to the cross shelter for our 'Christmas dinner' we were surprised to find half a dozen others there already and our dream of a 'people free summit' vanished into the still air. They had come up from Wythburn and they welcomed us with hearty cries of "Merry Christmas" so it was hard to resent their presence. We went into an empty bay of the shelter and had just reached the mince pie stage of proceedings when a party of pensioners staggered over the summit having arrived in a mini-bus at Thirlspot below. They were really into the Christmas theme and tinsel was in abundance. They were a great bunch, the oldest was in his mid-seventies and they said they did this sort of thing every year. So much for empty fells on Christmas Day!

We departed as the party really got going – drawing the line at singing chorus after chorus of 'Jingle Bells', so we left them too it. It wasn't late and realising we had made too good time to the top we retired to Lower Man to sit and soak up the atmosphere. We had hoped to descend in the dusk but there was no way you could sit around for another two hours in that freezing air so we set off for Swirral Edge.

My abiding memory of the descent was arriving at the ice plastered cairn and looking down Swirral Edge at a wonderful iced up ridge and wondering how I was going to get down it as my left crampon had just snapped clean in half at the front base plate. The first twenty feet or so are the nasty bit here and after that most of the awkward spots can be avoided. The solution was simple in the end. My wife climbed down the tricky top bit and took a length of our rope with her. She tied her crampons to it and I hauled them back and used them. We had to do it in a few other places before we reached the safety of Red Tarn and I missed out some of the better parts of the ridge, but it was still a fantastic day.

The year after was a complete contrast. Foolishly we agreed to camp at the 'all year' site near the head of Great Langdale. It seemed a good idea as the Old and New Dungeon Ghyll pubs were both within staggering distance. We arrived on the afternoon of Christmas Eve and stayed too late in the New Dungeon Ghyll that night. Not surprisingly we were the only ones at the camp site and Christmas Day dawned grey but mild and saw us heading off late nursing hangovers.

A planned route up Scafell Pike was abandoned in favour of a circuit of Bowfell and Esk Pike which seemed easier. We really did have the hills to ourselves that day, and by the time we neared the top of The Band, bits of blue sky began to show and on the summit of Bowfell, with our Christmas Day picnic spread around us, the sun was out and the clouds high and wispy. We had the fell top to ourselves that day with no other parties to interfere with our plans, and two things have stuck in my mind down the years. The first was how mild it was. There was little wind, the sun was warm and we lingered long on the top lounging in short sleeves and slowly recovering from the previous night.

The second was our descent. By the time we got over Esk Pike and down to Esk Hause the dusk was turning to night and our descent of Rossett Gill was done by head torch in complete darkness. The sky had stayed clear and it was surprisingly still mild, so we took our time lingering on the walk out along Mickleden. It was magical and after a few well-earned drinks at the Old Dungeon Ghyll we finally staggered back to our tents.

Perhaps the most memorable of all our Christmas Day adventures was, oddly enough, the last one we ever did. Again it was with friends and there was the usual tinsel and hats, but for some reason I can't remember we set off very late from Ambleside in freezing conditions with snow deep on the tops to do the Fairfield Horseshoe. We were very slow. I seem to recall we were all fairly exhausted as it had been a hard working run up to the festive season. Lunch was had on High Pike and we took far too long over it. We finally reached Fairfield as dusk was falling. None of us had the energy or the inclination to continue in the dark so we backtracked to the col between Fairfield and Hart Crag and did a swift descent down the snow into Rydale. Although none of us had been that way before, it looked straight forward enough on the map. We picked up a frozen cart track on the valley floor as complete darkness fell and the temperature plummeted. It was tricky walking as any standing water had frozen but it was impractical to wear crampons, so we had to be very careful not to go flying if we didn't spot the slippery stuff. Seeing anything was the main problem we had. We had been careless in our preparations and had only three head torches in the party. Problem was they all had old batteries in them and the freezing temperatures soon saw two of them off. Mine lasted a bit longer, but not long enough and none of us had been sensible enough to pack a spare. It really was a pitch black night and we groped our way down Rydale keeping Rydal Beck to our right. Night vision never really kicked in, there were numerous falls and much cursing and often the sound of waterfalls seemed far too close for comfort. Although it was frightening, we were a lot younger and the party all experienced and in a perverse way, we all enjoyed it.

As we entered trees someone spotted what looked like conifers across the narrowing beck, so we carefully crossed and pushed a way through them thinking they meant civilisation. Crossing a low fence we found ourselves on a well cut lawn and suddenly illuminated by several high power security lights. We had inadvertently stumbled into the grounds of Rydal Hall and expected to be jumped by burly security guards with drooling dogs at any moment. But, hey, it was Christmas, everyone was having the day off and absolutely nothing happened. So we hastily exited and we finally gained the main road and marched back into Ambleside in a great party mood waving at the odd car that passed us by and honked. Even if you think it isn't your cup of tea, try giving a Christmas Day fell walk a go one year. You may be surprised at the memories you get left with!

And if you think that is too much and I must need a good shrink, it only gets worse – how about spending New Year's Eve on a Lakeland hillside? On the surface it sounds like a barmy idea but routine can be a dreary thing and a change really is as good as a rest.

We spent last New Year on the Caravan Club site at Troutbeck Head under the slopes of Great Mell Fell. It's perhaps a sign of advancing age that we sought the luxury of a heated van over the freezing interior of a small tent during the Christmas break, but there it was. We took some outdoor lights (Santa and a snowman) for the kids and we had a lovely time and were able to get out on the fells for all of the four days of our stay. The passage of time became an issue on New Year's Eve when we met up with our friends Kenny and his wife Sarah on the roadside near Calebrack by the ford over Carrock Beck, north of Mungrisedale. Our planned route over Carrock Fell and High Pike was a leisurely affair with lots of reminiscing about days long gone and a heated debate as to the exact date of the last time we had done this particular route together. All parties finally agreed it had been over ten years before. Ten years! Not only had we been a decade younger then but a lifetime sillier and at the pub later that evening the conversation turned to New Year's Eves of the past and the distances backward became even greater. There had been a regular group of us in our younger years and various daft ventures had been our trademark. One of our crazier ideas was to spend New Year's Eve on a mountain top and 'first foot' the fells before anyone else could. Sounds daft now and the first attempt, on Ben Nevis of all places, was an out and out failure with gale force winds and driving rain falling on frozen snow and beating us back a long way before the summit plateau, but the idea had gripped one or two of us and the following year we organised the slightly saner option of trying the same thing but on Great Gable in the Lakes.

The theory was simple enough. It was not to be an overnight stop; we needed a top we all knew well, lots of food, and plenty of head torches with spare batteries. We would ascend and descend by different routes in the dark and spend the final half hour of the old year and the first half hour of the new on the summit. A few celebration drinks were planned once we got back down, but as it would be well into the wee hours by then, we didn't expect this to go on for very long.

Gable from Wasdale was a good choice – we all knew it very well, it was rough and would demand respect in the dark and the route finding would be far from straightforward. And it was a true mountain summit to spend any night on, but in particular a special one such as New Year's Eve. There was even a small camp site facing Ritson's Bar at the Wasdale Head Inn which suited us fine as we were all a lot poorer then and besides, anyone suggesting such a luxury as a hotel room for a few nights would have been laughed at and branded a wimp! We fared better that year with the weather, there was little wind and no lying snow, but one of those fine drizzly rains fell on and off for most of the night and when it came the clag dropped making walking by head torch hard as the beam tended to bounce back in your face. Anyway, to cut the story short, a party of seven of us climbed up to Sty Head and then up the Breast Route to the summit of Gable. There were two things I remember clearly from that first night, the first was the lights we saw from two or three tents by Sty Head Tarn – there was no noise from them but as least we weren't the only lunatics out on the hills in the dark. And the second was how cold it was on the summit of Great Gable. It was a mild night overall, but once we stopped and opened up flasks and chocolate, all of us, without exception, began to shiver. The head torches went off and it truly was pitch black with no stars and our eyes never really adjusted to the night.

We counted the New Year in as close as we could using our watches, the men shook hands and took it in turns to hug the girls, and we set off down the other side of the mountain to pick up the Moses Trod path and descend back to Wasdale. There was nothing of great incident to report as we went back and Wasdale Head was silent when we arrived at almost half past three. We quietly toasted the success of the venture with more drinks and planned something similar for the following year.

And although for one reason or another it never happened the next New Year's Eve, it set a precedent and over the years that followed we undertook the same lunacy several times, always in a group and nearly always in the Lakes – although we did one trip up Snowdon in North Wales which was an epic adventure due to ice and snow near the top.

The strangest New Year I ever spent on a Lake District summit was on top of Glenridding Dodd of all places. Our intended destination had been Helvellyn but two days of gales had battered the Lakes and we knew it would be foolish to climb it at night in such weather. Having come prepared to spend a night on the summit on this occasion, we were reluctant to not try something, but I have no idea now how we agreed on this lowly top.

It turned out to be a great night even though it was windy. Setting out from Glenridding late in the evening – we made it a point not to go to the pub before these ventures so as to keep clear heads – we arrived on the summit a good hour before midnight, spread out roll mats and got (fully dressed) into sleeping bags covered in plastic survival sacks (bivvy bags being beyond our budgets at that time!).

Using rucksacks to lean on we sat in the dark, passed a bottle of whisky around (or maybe two!) and saw in the New Year. We had brought a picnic of sorts and shared a decent feast before collapsing and sleeping until dawn when the intense cold finally drove us back down to a still sleeping Glenridding.

There have been other nights too. We camped on Blencathra on a still freezing night near the white cross in the saddle and watched a shower of shooting stars fall from a clear sky an hour after the New Year had arrived. We slept late the next day providing much amusement to the numerous walkers who arrived on the summit for a New Year's outing.

There was an unplanned ascent of Catbells with two East German lads we had met at a pub in Keswick when we arrived at the summit far too early and were already back at Hawse End as New Year arrived! And for me, one of the strangest incidents of all was standing on top of Skiddaw on a drizzly New Year's Eve many years ago, talking to a man I couldn't see about places we had climbed in the Alps. A party of us had planned the trip around the fact the weather was forecast to be cold and clear over the late December period. It was around the time that fireworks on New Year's Eve had become the big thing to do and the noise and sight of them, looking down from above was sensational. Anyway, we had the idea of sitting atop Skiddaw and watching the fireworks below as a novel way of seeing in another New Year. It never happened. We set off in a frosty clear air only to arrive on the summit ridge in thick clag and drizzle which never lifted. For the first time ever we had company on the top in the form of two other men and it was with one of those I discussed climbing days and routes. We heard the fireworks below as the New Year arrived but saw nothing. I never knew this chap's name but we spent half an hour making friends and by the time we left we knew a lot about each other but I never really saw his face in the gloom. They were staying on the top for the night and we left them to it and if the gentleman concerned is reading this, I hope he enjoyed our little chat as much as I did!

All these memories came about because of a reunion in the northern fells. This year I will have my caravan at the Camping and Caravanning Club site at Windermere and will no doubt enjoy the heating, the T.V. with live football and the comfort, but my kids are getting older now and my thoughts are already turning to a few mad cap ideas for the future – that is if I can cope with the discomfort and cold after all these years of soft living!

The dark nights of winter seem to go on for ever but when spring hits Cumbria it can be magical. New plans are formed and a new lease of life seems to arrive in my body and soul. It has to be my favourite season of the year, especially the latter months of it when the leaves have the fresh green colour about them and the daylight seems to last for ever.

And of all months, I guess there is one that stands out above all others on the fells for me and that is the truly magnificent month of May.

Spring – An Ode to May

That May is my favourite Lakeland month will come as no surprise to those who know me. The memories of sunny mornings, cloudless skies and leaving Keswick on a launch over the lake to head up Catbells and onwards with hours of daylight ahead are always strong in my mind.

Wordsworth, in his *Ode to May* says:

'All nature welcomes her whose sway
Tempers the year's extremes
Who scattereth lustres o'er noonday
Like morning's dewy gleams'

Everyone welcomes the arrival of May with the delights of bright green leaves on trees, blossom and long long days. But to be fair, the poet's 'May vision' probably only visits us once or twice every ten years nowadays with our weather being so upside down. Last May was wet and windy as we ploughed through thick snow on a late month Munro bagging session in Scotland.

However, when we get a perfect May in the Lake District the pleasures we experience live with us for the rest of our lives. If I close my eyes and think of warm May days it is not just Keswick that comes to mind. The memories of Buttermere and Ennerdale in late May are strong too. Ennerdale in particular, sparkling in bright May sunshine with the Lake twinkling and dancing in a light breeze and that endless skyline of fells circling around and beckoning the walker onwards is a favourite daydream on wild winter nights at home or sat in some remote pub by a roaring fire after a bitter day on the tops.

Ennerdale is one of those valleys that seem to grasp the best of every season and display it for all to see. In autumn it can be ablaze with colours and in the darker months it is the epitome of Lakeland winter scenes with iron looking fells in barren winters and snow topped ones under perfect blue skies in harsh ones – which we see so few of nowadays. Perhaps I have a rose-tinted perspective here, but if we only get such conditions occasionally, they surely characterise to us what our perfect Lakeland is and we should dwell long on such thoughts.

Going back to May, the visions I have of perfect days are now planted irrevocably in my soul and will always be associated with that month. True, it makes me suffer great disappointment when a wet and windy year wipes out the dream, but when a 'Wordsworthian' one comes along then I am ready to drop all commitments and relish its wonders.

And so, Ennerdale, a valley in which I had one of my strangest Lakeland experiences one mid-May Monday. My wedding anniversary falls in May and my wife and I have always celebrated it by choosing an area of the Lakes and just heading off to spend some days amongst the fells there. On the anniversary in question we had stayed at the Youth Hostel at Gillerthwaite the night before and were headed with backpacks over to Wasdale for the next night, our intention being to take in Pillar and anything else we fancied on the way. It was, of course, a wonderful May morning.

I love the walk up Ennerdale, and the circuit of the lake has always been one of my favourite low level routes in Lakeland. I have to admit too, that the long horseshoe around the fells surrounding the Lake – the Ennerdale Skyline Walk – is a challenge for a fit walker and ranks highly on my list of 'best Lake District days'.

The day in question saw us in no particular hurry, we had hours of daylight ahead of us and it has always been our custom to linger on the tops until late in the day to enjoy them in the stillness of evening when the crowds have left.

As we walked up the track towards the Black Sails hut at the head of the dale we became aware of a rustling movement in the trees to our left. Whatever it was it sounded big and we instantly thought 'deer' and we stopped so as not to scare it. The noise stopped too and we discussed whether we had ever seen a deer in Ennerdale or knew anyone who had. We didn't think so and as nothing else happened we thought we must have 'spooked' it so we carried on.

Immediately the movement started again – a distinct heavy rustling in the trees to our left as though something big was moving alongside us but out of sight. And so it went on. We stopped, it stopped. We went through the various creatures it could have been apart from deer, and judging by the sound we guessed the size to be fox, sheep, cow or dog. It has to be said that we are veterans of many nights spent on lonely mountain tops and we don't scare easily, but this was beginning to bother us somewhat. It was a week day and there was nobody else around and we began to wonder about the possibility of a human stalking us – you know how your mind works in these situations – escaped convict, chainsaw killer, that sort of thing!

Stopping, we headed into the trees to see if we could catch a glimpse of whatever it was. The noise stopped again too. It was a still day with little wind so we would have heard whatever it was if it scuttled away but all was still. This 'stand off' between us and our unseen foe continued even as the trees thinned and only ceased when we reached clear open ground. We never saw anything at all and I would be lying if I said that our pace didn't increase dramatically the longer it went on. However, with the glories of upper Ennerdale basking in the midday May sun we soon forgot all about it and headed up to the Black Sails Pass.

On the way up Pillar we met an old boy with a bushy white beard eating his butties, passed the time of day and then spent the next six hours meandering from fell to fell with no set purpose apart from finally arriving to camp at Wasdale that night. Sunburnt and exhausted we walked from our tent to Ritson's Bar at the Wasdale Head Inn late in the evening and there we met the old boy with the bushy beard again. It was a quiet night in Ritson's and we got into conversation with him about the day we had had. As the drinks flowed we told him about our stranger encounter in the Ennerdale woods.

Without hesitation he said, "that'll have been the ghost of t'girt dog of Ennerdale, I've heard of that happening to people before". He turned out to be fairly local to the area (somewhere along the coast if memory serves me correctly) and a mine of information and I will recount the story of this strange dog to you as he told it to us in case you haven't heard it before.

'T 'girt dog of Ennerdale' appeared for the first time in May 1816 and became known locally as 'The Ennerdale Vampire' as well as by his more usual name. Mangled sheep began to appear in Lower Ennerdale but at this time this was far from unusual as wild dogs were common. Usually they were killed within days of their arrival but 't 'girt dog' was different. No one saw him, no trace could be found of him, he never seemed to visit the same area twice on his raids and the area he terrorised was widespread with attacks often being as much as twenty miles apart. Fear spread amongst the locals and terrifying stories of supernatural beings kept the children indoors at night or shaking with fear as they walked to school in the morning. The death toll increased as the carcasses mounted up and although he seemed to work exclusively at night, there were odd sightings of him in the mornings by shepherds and the descriptions of a hell hound of enormous size with fire lit eyes became more exaggerated as the days went by. That summer was one of sheer terror for the residents of Ennerdale. Shooting parties would stake out an area for the dog only for him to mount an attack miles away. It was as though he knew what his hunters were up to. Often wild dogs such as this moved on after a while but by September his blood lust was still growing and he seemed to have settled into the area for good. A bounty was put on his head and the area filled with hunters. But the dog eluded fox hounds, stayed away from the guns and began to expand his territory taking in Cockermouth and St Bees on the coast. After a chase involving over two hundred men the great beast was finally killed in mid-September and his body was stuffed and set up in Keswick Museum with a collar around his neck describing his exploits.

Ennerdale returned to peace. Well, not quite, if my informant was anything to go by as the monster's spirit still roamed the area! I don't believe in ghosts! I don't know what we heard that May day but I did a bit of research into Lakeland's own 'Hound of the Baskervilles' and his story was true. But nothing could ruin May for me – not even some spectral hound stalking me up one of my favourite valleys.

May is Lakeland at its best and is there to be enjoyed by all who love such things. But it can be a fleeting occurrence and you need to be ready to react in an instant to a good forecast and be off with boots and rucksack packed – or it can be gone for another twelve months!

And after May comes our summer, so longed for and so looked forward to, but as I mentioned earlier it can be a let down some years – certainly for the last decade many summers have followed the familiar and distressing pattern of being warm and damp and the fells have brooded under low cloud. Very disappointing when we have expected so much and anticipated much better for so long, but things are never so bad as we think they are and an early morning saunter on the tops or a late evening in July can reap many rewards as you either get out before the weather sets in or are heading out as it clears from the west as it so often does in Lakeland.

Summer – Lakeland's Early Morning Mountains

Experiencing the sun rising out of the mist on a delightful early summer morning off a Lakeland summit is a fascinating and enchanting way to begin a day amongst the fells. It may sound a strange thing to want to do but ask any professional mountain photographer the best time to get stunning images and he will advocate a pre-dawn start to the day whatever the season. The joys that can be yours if you forsake your bed in the small hours and head for the hills have to be experienced to be believed. On the surface the thought of dragging yourself up a steep path at somewhere between two and three in the pre-dawn hours can seem very unappealing. I felt similarly until I boldly stepped out and rubbed the sleep from my eyes and gave it a go.

Let me share that day with you and then take you through my

own progression into this absorbing and addictive way to enjoy our Lakeland tops. I saw it initially as a Lakeland summer pastime but as you will see I have advanced to other seasons too – but make no mistake, summer is still probably the best time for doing it. And like numerous others, the first time I looked hopefully eastwards at a rapidly lightening skyline was from the flat summit of Helvellyn.

A non-hill walking friend had a daughter in her mid-twenties who badgered me to take her up this mountain as she wanted to be a part of the annual pilgrimage to the top and watch the sun rise over the Pennines on the longest day of the year. Traditionally, hundreds of people crowd onto the summit here every 21 June to see the sun appear. Some come for the atmosphere, some hoping for a spiritual experience and others, like me, to see what all the fuss is about. Cloud and clag often prevent them from seeing much and turn the whole outing into a shivering, miserable experience. However, I allowed myself to be talked into the outing.

We set off from Glenridding at midnight to give us plenty of time to get to the top before sunrise that we knew would be between four and five in the morning. I thought we would be on our own, but we soon took our place in a long line of other hopefuls climbing towards Keppel Cove; it was a clear night with a good moon and after a while our eyes adjusted quite well to the low light. The summit was fairly packed, some had bivouacked in the cross shelter and groups formed with much good natured bantering taking place. Flasks were plentiful and I felt a little out of place amongst it all.

However, we had not rushed to get up, and it was only about half an hour of sharing a flask and butties before the sky to the east rapidly started to become lighter and then Lakeland began to appear out of the darkness. There was no mist, no cloud, no wind and the sky was a deep blue – it was going to be a hot day and we were out on the high hills right at the start of it.

The sun was not the great red ball I had expected as it rose over the Pennines, more a golden orb that seemed to turn the eastern horizon a hundred different flashes of brilliance. There was some 'oohhhhing' and 'ahhhing', one or two of the more spiritual types raised arms and closed eyes but mostly a profound silence fell over the gathered masses.

And then it was over and we all moved off, most heading back down – my intention had been to get my own back on my walking companion Susan for keeping me up all night by taking her down Striding Edge, but she out did me and sprang a surprise of her own on me. She had arranged for her dad to collect us on the A66 near Threlkeld so we could traverse the ridge all the way north to Clough Head! "Of course," she said as the summit emptied, "if it's a little much for you at your age...." Well of course we did her route and although she bought me a nice meal in the evening, I spent most of the time asleep drooling onto my fleece!

I have never returned to Helvellyn to see the sunrise but I have repeated the experience on many other Lakeland mountains numerous times since and at all times of the year. I have done it alone and in company and I have to say, that apart from that one experience outlined above, I have never shared the summits at daybreak with another party (apart from the one I was with) except for once, and that was on Blencathra on a December day when we had a very memorable sunrise.

Still not convinced? Think of it like this – you get onto the tops before the crowds at the start of the day and are often on your way down well before the first of the day visitors are half way up the main paths. There is also the added bonus of seeing one of nature's wonderful natural phenomena. The down side is having to get up very early and you need to plan well and watch the weather closely. There is absolutely no point going on dodgy forecasts as you're wasting your time – even the good ones can let you down!

I remember a group of us sweating our way up the Long Stile Ridge to High Street because Michael Fish predicted clear skies and being highly frustrated as we were met by high winds, rain and zero visibility! But get it right (or fall lucky) and it will be one of the best mountain experiences of all for you. You have to be prepared for disappointment, but the more you watch the weather patterns, the better your chances of being stood up high with jaw dropped open wondering why people worry about such mundane things as work when you can see a sight like this for free!

As for the practical side of the matter, either you do the start in the dark or you stay overnight on the top. The latter is a great option for the late spring and summer when it gets light a few hours after going dark. A Lakeland summit on a summer night can be enchanting, but expect it to be cold and take a bivvy bag with plenty of warm clothing and flasks.

Often you're better getting up early and plodding through the dark to a summit you know well – there's nothing more frustrating than wasting that early start by getting lost on unfamiliar territory. It's best, of course, if you are experienced with map and compass and not afraid of mountain territory in dark conditions. It can be surprising just how scary a familiar, well known path can appear at night and landmarks seen many times in daylight can be missed or appear totally different in darkness. Take my advice and do it with friends; alone it is an eerie experience but with the company of others the walk up passes quickly in good humoured chat and it can be surprising how long you seem to have to wait for dawn once you get there. The dark seems to fight a battle with the daylight and reluctantly gives way. It can be cold even in July and August, so make sure you are well wrapped up with plenty of coffee and grub.

It's worth giving it a go in spring and autumn too once you get the hang of it – autumn in particular can treat you to some real 'other worldly' sunrise experiences as the misty mornings give you blood red orbs struggling into pale blue skies. It will be cool, but delicious. Spring can be cold but the clarity on early frosty mornings is amazing – however beware of icy paths and the associated dangers especially in darkness.

And as to where the best place to watch a sunrise from is, there is a great deal of choice in the Lakes. Helvellyn always gets mentioned and because of its great height is very good indeed – but give midsummer's night a miss! The eastern fells have a distinct advantage of course, but any high ground with a good view east will suffice. A good access path, not too much bad terrain and a nice summit for sitting it out on are all prerequisites. There needs to be plenty of places to lounge – rocks, a nice sheltered cairn, that sort of thing. And make sure it is a place you like. Familiarity does not breed contempt on this occasion.

Skiddaw is good and Blencathra is probably better but harder to climb in the dark. I like High Street and Kidsty Pike, but most of the higher fells of the Lakes will suffice – there are plenty where modern man has probably never climbed to watch the sunrise. Use your maps, look for the height first of all and the view east. Use your Wainwright's *Pictorial Guide* – he was excellent on views and will point you in the right direction; but most of all, use your own experience. If you have walked the Lakeland summits you will already be forming ideas in your mind. Put these plans into action. Get a few friends together, set a day and begin to track the weather patterns. It will be time well spent and will open up a whole new era to your love affair with mountain Lakeland.

And as the year gets old and we move into autumn I have to say I love the earlier months of this particular season. It is one time of the year that has a great peace about it with often still, smoky, days and the crisp leaves falling from a mellow sky under a warm sun. It's a shame that September is a forerunner of greyer days and colder shorter nights as it would certainly challenge May as a favourite month of mine if it didn't. But putting that aside, you can't take anything away from a proper Lakeland autumn day and the joy of kicking though crisp brown leaves as a silky dusk falls and the lure of a café and cake at day's end is hard to resist.

But as we are looking at quirkier sides of Lakeland days, how about the 'off' days when you find the late season winds blowing and the conditions less than perfect? How many times have you made the effort to get to the foot of the fells and found that the wind is gusting too much or the rain looks ominous on an October morning? There is many an autumn day I have spent on the fells in these conditions and enjoyed beyond belief – it's all a question of perspective and being smart.

Autumn – When the North Wind does Blow

Late September to late November is an unsettled time on the Lakeland fells and the wind can be a nuisance as the autumn takes hold and begins to give us a taste of the winter to come; but during all my years climbing these tops I have only really been blown off my feet twice so we often make more of blowy conditions than we need to. However, there is no point being stupid and taking chances in wild conditions and, although I dream of a golden autumn in the same way I fantasise about a white Christmas, the reality is often a windy or wet October day, and often both.

So what do you do in those circumstances? Well, I guess the obvious answer is to avoid them, but that's not always possible is it? All regular hill goers watch the weather avidly on the days leading up to a walk and if you are like me, you are constantly checking websites, webcams and updated Met Office reports and warnings.

Plans are changed and adapted so as to accommodate our strange climate and get the best from limited leisure time. So perhaps it is no surprise I have not suffered at the hands of the wind as much as I could have.

The last thing you want to do is get it wrong and end up climbing up something and regretting it afterwards as it was unpleasant or potentially dangerous. Make no mistake; a strong wind on higher ground could easily be a killer. As I mentioned before I have been blown off my feet twice in almost a quarter of a century of Lakeland fell walking but the two times in question were frightening enough. The first was actually not in autumn but was on a New Year's Day on Stile End between Outerside and Barrow and I was on my own. It had been very windy all night and I just fancied a short route to see in the New Year, so setting off early from Braithwaite I climbed up Outerside and headed along the ridge. It was useless and dangerous with it. The wind howled and was that nasty sort that comes in unexpected gusts. I decided to abandon the attempt on Stile End and drop down the front steeply to gain the sanctuary of Braithwaite again. Just as I left the summit a gust hit me from behind and lifted me clean into the air and dumped me bruised and shaken 15 feet down the fell side. That has happened to me in Snowdonia on the 3,000 footers before (including one memorable time on the Glyders when a party of four of us were bowled into the air like skittles and dumped in several different places well away from each other) but not in Lakeland.

The second time was more recent and my own fault. On a day of early blizzards and gales in late November my wife and I set out to climb Skiddaw. Just up and down the Jenkins Hill path, nothing fancy as the weather was so awful, but we had arranged babysitters and taken the time to get there so it seemed a shame to waste it. We coped with the wind until the final climb to the south summit and the ridge to the trig point. There it became very wild. A scared looking party passed us coming down with dire warnings about attempting to go any further as it was just too bad. In our defence it has to be said we have climbed and walked in many parts of the world and would consider ourselves experienced in most conditions having made some fairly epic descents in foul weather over the years. It seemed like a challenge and we decided to take up the gauntlet.

But our new friends had been right. Standing on the summit ridge was nigh on impossible and the only way to make progress was to cling on to each other and sort of shuffle in a crouched position holding each other up. We made the summit (it had been fairly scary to say the least) and after huddling for a bit of shelter near the trig and getting some coffee and chocolate into us, we braced ourselves for the return journey.

Now, as often happens in these situations, the wind had increased during our brief stop and was now up to somewhere around storm force. Thankfully the clouds had cleared and the blizzards gone but even the wonderful visibility did little to compensate for that awful half mile we had to endure to get off. Twice we were blown off our feet, once was near the summit and the bruise on the bottom of my back from the resulting 'dumping down' lasted weeks. Forward progress was only possible by crawling. We were fast losing body heat and in lots of trouble. We stopped, huddled close and took stock of our situation. It was a westerly wind so we half crawled, half rolled off the ridge and descended east down the rough slopes. It took about 200 feet of descent before we felt safe again and the wind became bearable. We had had enough of Skiddaw for one day so we headed down over Sale How and returned via the track to Skiddaw House and under Lonscale Fell.

So how do you avoid unpleasant experiences like this? Well,

quite simply, you adapt your route to cheat the wind. Over the years we have developed several routes on fells that we now call 'windy day hills'. A lot of these came about because we often took our kids into the hills and we obviously needed to make the days we spent there both safe and enjoyable for them. But with a bit of practice it is not hard to follow what we did and 'grab' a hill day when it seems like it is a lost cause and you are about to write off yet another autumn day.

The first thing to realise is obvious – the wind strength always increases as you ascend. So when you get out of the car park at Seathwaite and the wind just about slams the car door in your face, maybe it's time to forget Scafell Pike for the day and try something a bit more moderate. It's surprising what 1,000 feet of altitude can do to weather. At 1,900 feet you may be able to stagger along while at 3,000 feet you would most likely become another mountain rescue statistic.

The other thing to look for in a windy day fell is lots of tree cover. Trees, particularly the thick coniferous ones that line many a Lakeland hill, are terrific at keeping bad weather off you. A storm tearing over high ground can sound deafening and frightening as you meander up a track through pine trees but you will hardly feel it hitting you. There is the problem of falling trees if it's proper storm force weather, but these are more likely to happen near forest edges where the tree line is exposed and anyway, if it really is storm force maybe you shouldn't be there at all – even on a sheltered route! The higher up the fell side the tree cover goes, the better. Many may have been the times we have cursed the march of plantations up our hills, but on the occasions we are looking at here, we need to be thankful for them. Being able to climb to almost 2,000 feet in bad weather is an advantage not to be scoffed at. The trees are a safety net for you because they don't really go much higher than 1,500 feet in the Lakes so you won't be tempted to risk really high routes. And if you chose wisely and go for a top that has a high tree line, you can make a quick dash for the summit and a hasty retreat into the shelter of the welcoming trees for protection again. Job done! You've bagged your top on a day when it looked unlikely you were going to get out of the car. The mileage may not be high and the route down simply a reversal of the way up, but look on the bright side, there are plenty of welcoming cafés waiting for you in Keswick or Ambleside.

There are a couple of things you need to bear in mind however, and I'm not trying to be a killjoy here, but they are important. The whole venture needs to be approached with a high degree of common sense. Even at lower altitudes wind can be highly dangerous, so if it is just too bad, don't even attempt it. If you get to the end of the forest and take a few steps into the open and get blown off your feet, get back into the trees and give it up for the day. And one obvious thing, your chosen forest needs to have a useable path through it up to the fell side. There is nothing harder and more disheartening than trying to force a way though coniferous trees without a path. Put simply, you will fail and get badly scratched.

And one final point, give the weather the respect it deserves. You may have cheated it by using a 'back door' route to the top, but never forget why you chose that way up. Wind can be a killer and as dangerous as snow, ice or rain. If you get blown off your feet and were to land wrong, well, I'll leave you to fill that bit in.

Get to your top, get back to shelter and keep a watchful eye on weather patterns once you are in the open. Don't linger or get your butties out on the summit.

No matter how experienced we were, our exploits on Skiddaw were probably not the most sensible thing we have ever done. We laugh about it now and remember it as a great adventure. Trust me, at the time, there wasn't a smile in sight – it was a horrifying experience. That being said, you can save wasted days by keeping a few lower and well protected routes up your sleeve. Here are some that have stood me in good stead:

RAVEN CRAG ABOVE THIRLMERE DAM: A mile up and a mile down and in trees with a good path all the way. Well protected but watch out for that summit and take care, it has a hell of a drop off it!

WHINLATTER: From the forest at the top of the pass a path zigzags up from near the end of the trees on the road to cross a stile and you leave the trees high on the ridge. A bit of a longer walk than I would normally like to get to the summit, but you have the trees to aim for to get back into shelter. Perhaps not the best for a really windy day.

CARRON CRAG: From the Grizedale Forest car park south of Hawkeshead. You are in trees almost all the way and the little rocky summit is quite a surprise and reminds you of much higher fells.

LORDS SEAT: Can be ascended along with Barf (miss it out and stay by the tree line if it is really windy) through the woods up Beckstones Gill or by using the new well made forest tracks that go nearly all the way to the top.

And if all else fails you could get five miles out of Claife Heights above Windermere from Far Sawrey. You'll get two tops and stay in trees almost all the time.

I feel sure that everyone who has read these lines will be able to slot other dates, times and experiences against this seasonal background of Lakeland fell life I have painted. There is so much variety here and all in so compact an area. It would be true to say that nowhere else in our country has such a variation of scenery and culture in so small a space. As I have said elsewhere, the effect on the eye is stunning and on the mind it is captivating.

Each person comes to this area in their own way. Some only walk here in the warmer months but many, like me, are, and always have been, year round visitors. And to be fair, as Lakeland has increased in popularity over the last decade and the fells have become busier, I have often preferred those off-season times and especially the mid-week period when fewer walkers are out on the tops and I can get away from civilisation, albeit for a short time. Even at that time of year and at that time of the week, there are very few days when you won't see someone else or even be able to look around you and not spot figures in the distance.

I am not anti-social by nature and often like the company of others on my routes, especially good friends of long standing. A decent friend will walk with you and companionable silences that often last for an hour or more as you both recall past days and times on the area you are walking through. Conversation is not an essential on a walk in the hills, but it's nice to be able to do it if you need to. Many would argue that an experience such as Lakeland gives is best savoured by sharing it with others and who am I to disagree? Like I have said all along, this is personal to each and every one of us.

SOME ENCHANTED EVENING

Before we go on to look at more specific areas of the Lakeland scene, I have one more suggestion for enjoying the fells – it's something I have done often and am always watching for windows in the weather that will give me the chance to do it again.

This adventure is walking at night and is surely the ultimate in a 'getting away from the crowds philosophy' but will probably make most people reading this wince with the thought. However, it's not as daunting as you may imagine and when you consider that the Lakeland Poet Samuel Taylor Colderidge was a fan of it close to 200 years ago, often striding along the Helvellyn Ridge by moonlight to walk from Keswick to Grasmere to visit his friends the Wordsworths, you will begin to see it has many merits. And the lack of other walkers is only one of them.

The Lake District is probably the best area in the United Kingdom to undertake this strange pastime of night time fell walking. The fells here are friendly and the towns and villages crowd close below them so you never feel too far away from civilisation even in the remoter areas. If you tried to follow in the footsteps of the late Bill Murray who had a soft spot for undertaking this on Scottish mountains, you could often be seven or more miles away from the nearest habitation for a lot of the time and that can be a scary experience for the unwary or the unprepared.

The Lake District gives a far friendlier stage than this for trying a selection of nocturnal wanderings. In my opinion one of Lakeland's greatest pleasures in the early twenty first century is heading up on to the fells late in the day and making a night of it before descending back to the valleys at first light or shortly after. The lights from the farmhouses and streets below look romantic and beautiful and are the only indication that you are not the last person left in the entire world.

Let's be clear what we're talking about. This is, and has to be, a well planned and carefully thought out expedition with great care given to route selection and due consideration given to weather and the phase of the moon. There is always much more daylight than you think, as you will find if you go out (as I am suggesting here) to purposely wait for dark to start a walk, and it can take longer than you ever considered possible for the last dregs of daylight to vanish from the western sky, particularly in mid-summer. I am not a great fan of starting after dark from a car park and heading up to the tops so prefer to be up at a high point as the light finally goes so as to have a leisurely cup of coffee long before last light and then start the whole thing with good companions in complete darkness. This is not a pastime to be undertaken alone, although I have to admit that I have on many occasions, but if the whole thing is shared with like minded friends then the joys and delights are doubled and the risks are reduced significantly.

You need to be warm and dress up rather than down even on an August night – it's surprising just how cold it can really get and sitting at a summit cairn and waiting for total darkness can seem to take for ever. Your eyes adapt to the fading light, and if the sky is clear the light lingers much longer higher up than it does in the towns below.

By now you are probably thinking me a downright accident waiting to happen and the public enemy number one of the various Mountain Rescue teams and if you are already wondering how irresponsible one man can get, it's just about to get worse when I tell you that this is something I practice in the Lakes in winter as well as the summer months.

In fact it has to be said that in many ways the practice is far more practical in the late autumn, winter and early spring than it is at other times of the year. The darkness comes quicker and earlier then and doesn't entail you having to spend most of the night out on the open hillside waiting for the light to go. The only drawback in winter and late autumn is that the length of darkness is considerable and you may have to come back down in total blackness rather than wait for the wonderful dawn you hope to see. The only alternatives to this are to start much later and ascend in darkness, do a much longer route and linger over it or bivouac on the top and carry all the gear to sleep out in a sheltered spot once the route is finished. The great thing about a planned bivouac is that you get the hills to yourself in the glories of an early morning – but be prepared for just how cold a winter's night on a fell top can be!

I am in good company with my love of night walking. Wainwright was fond of this practice too and as our Lakeland hills become more and more crowded, it is one way to be able to still get the summit and ridges to yourself. And you get quite a superior feeling heading down a popular path after doing a ten mile route with the great clear views that only early morning can give you in the summer and passing the hordes of sweating day walkers on their way up.

This is a light hearted idea but I would never advocate irresponsible behaviour on the hills and particularly not in fading light. To enjoy this in the way it is intended will require some sound planning on your part – it's not just a question of meandering around in darkness and hoping for the best. First it's always a good thing to work out your timings. Where do you intend to be as the light goes and what do you intend to do afterwards? I usually head up late in the afternoon when others are starting to come down. It's surprising how fast the tops clear at that time of the day so be prepared to be alone very quickly. I have a route in mind and the length will depend on what time of the year it is. For instance, in early spring (when it is still dark for the best part of twelve hours) a round of Coledale from Causey Pike, over Sail and Eel Crags and even taking a detour off Hopegill Head to Ladyside Pike before arriving on Grisedale Pike will take you five hours or so on a moonlit night with no snow and ice but maybe an hour or two longer in full winter conditions. As the descent path is excellent from Grisedale Pike you will then be able to follow it back to Braithwaite with the lights of Keswick below you and Derwentwater looking like a black blot on the scenery or glimmering in moonlight if you are lucky enough to have it; or you can bivvy somewhere near the plantations on Kinn after the descent of Sleet How and wait until first light to do the same thing.

There are no rules to this particular fell game – you tailor it to suit yourself and your companions and it changes every time you do it.

The constants are safety, time spent on the tops and available moonlight which is the most important aspect of all. A good moonlit night is almost as good as walking in daylight and the effects are purely magical. All the Lakeland tops will be laid out in eerie half light around you and the only thing missing will be other people.

Factor in the seasonality and you should be in for a memorable experience. The idea is to traverse familiar tops during the hours of darkness and preferably at the period on or around the full moon with a good clear night in prospect and with a good path to follow. You can vary this idea to incorporate most fell days, but always, always, aim to be at a known and familiar point at last light to give yourself the best possible start. And take into account the weather as well. You want good clear conditions to get the most out of it. Call the whole thing off if it is murky or raining. The real glory of this is a sky full of stars, a great blob of a moon and the lakes spread out below.

My very best Lakeland hill memory was of a winter's night circuit around the Newlands tops. The fells were covered in frozen snow and we had a full moon and clear sky. It was like walking in an eerie daylight and no torches were needed. It was not an accidental occurrence; we had planned it and postponed it once already waiting for the right conditions. Once we reached Hindscarth we turned around and went back again over Dale Head and the High Spy Ridge finishing with breakfast in Keswick. This is generally beyond the scope of regular night time hill walking and a darkness traverse of frozen ground is not for the faint hearted. Avoid trying such outings unless you have general mountaineering experience and can give yourself plenty of time.

So let's assume you have a route in mind, a point you aim to be at when dusk comes and you have watched the weather and moon carefully. Other key things are to make sure you choose reliable companions and check your gear in advance. Don't forget things such as spare batteries for the head torch and an extra flask with some grub for that first and last summit. I am stressing the safety aspect of this venture heavily – go prepared and you will have memories that linger long, if you don't, it will be an unpleasant experience and potentially dangerous too.

Whether you choose to go for long routes or just to snatch a short fell walk in some limited time available to you during a busy life, make sure you give it a go and extend your enjoyment of the wonderful Lakeland hills. If you are serious about searching for a 'Lost Lakeland' experience you probably can't get much better than this. It has a true wilderness and adventure feeling about it and will have you coming back time and time again to give it another go when the full moon is forecast.

Changing the subject a little I feel that it's very common for all of us to single out the big summits, the largest rounds and the epic scrambles to the exclusion of all else. I have mentioned fitting as much as we could into our busy lives by simply going at obscure times and expanding the available hours to fit around our days.

Although it is in principal the thing to do, we have to balance it with a bit of common sense or we will miss out on so much and begin to neglect and despise the things we see as lesser objects for our endeavours. Before I finish this chapter I will show you what I mean by taking a look at one of those summits seen often by motorists on the A66 and by visitors to Keswick as they gaze up from its streets. Poor old Latrigg has much to offer the walker but many serious fell goers would never admit to going out for a day on its lowly slopes. It's too easy, too small, not challenging enough, the same argument which can be applied to lots of the more humble of Lakeland summits. And yet someone fills up those car parks below them and makes those distinct paths to the top. If it is neither you nor I, then I wonder just who it could be?

HEAVEN IN THE HILLS

To finish this chapter I want to show you how much you could be missing by craning your neck ever upwards and having an interest only in the higher and what are often considered, more demanding, summits of the Lake District.

It's pretty rare to get the summit ridge to yourself on Latrigg. I suppose I have climbed this little hill on dozens of occasions, probably more than most others in the Lake District, and I can still only recall once when I was alone on the top.

It was a blustery late March evening just before the clocks went forward and the light nights returned. I had been dropped by a friend at the entrance to the farm track a couple of miles from Bassenthwaite Village and had enjoyed a great winter's day traverse of Skiddaw ascending via Dash Falls, Bakestall and the north ridge. There had been enough snow to justify the ice axe and winter gear I had been carrying and there were plenty of people around the trig point on Skiddaw's summit. It has always been my habit to linger late on summits and let the crowds disperse and this happened a lot quicker than I anticipated on that particular day as a nasty little wind blew up and made the half mile trek along the frozen skyline summit ridge a bit exciting to say the least. On the south top you could barely stand up but as I dropped it eased and a wonderful evening settled over the north lakes. By the time I reached the car park between Skiddaw and Latrigg it was still and mellow. I had about an hour before total darkness and I decided to include Latrigg in my descent to Keswick. There was no snow this low down but the grass was yellow after the long winter as I climbed up the path towards the top. There had been one or two cars still lingering in the parking area and I had expected people to be up there but what a surprise awaited me on my arrival.

I love coming up this way. A dull grassy slope suddenly gives way to one of the Lakes' most amazing views as Derwentwater and the range of fells that surround it leap into view. From Helvellyn, Dow Crag and Crinkle Crags to the left and centre, the panorama swings through a feast of fantastic mountains to Scafell Pike, Scafell and Great Gable to your right and slightly west. And in between and closer to you, Catbells, Dale Head, the Jaws of Borrowdale, Rosthwaite Fell, Glaramara and Grange Fell are laid out as a backdrop against the islands of Derwentwater and the streets of Keswick below.

The clarity of the air that evening was stunning meaning you could see for many miles, and what was even better was that I was totally alone. I lingered long on that wonderful ridge playing name the fell as I moved my eyes around the impressive skyline. It was pretty much dark when I left but I couldn't have cared less. It was pure heaven up there that night. I love late March anyway. The winter is behind us and the weather is just starting to give a few hints of what lies ahead. The daylight hangs on until almost seven o' clock and you know summer is just around the corner. And to be in that sublime place alone was utopia. I was not the only one who thought this lowly summit was heavenly. Our old friend Alfred Wainwright had the following to say about Latrigg and its all encompassing view – "will there be mountains like these in Heaven, or is this Heaven before death?"

He had a point! Latrigg is one of those mountains many of us have used as a face saver over the years. If all else failed you could always do a quick ascent from the car park at the top of the Gale Road no matter what the weather and it beats going home summit less on rough days. But I would defy anyone to say that once they had done this once they did not return to this top to savour some of the other ways up it. It may be small but it packs a mighty punch in the view stakes. If you have never used it as a way to and from Skiddaw may I recommend you give it a try at least once. It makes a great extension to the route and finishes the day off with the most amazing descent back down to Keswick.

However, I feel Latrigg has enough character of its own to be chosen as a hill for a day's fell walking in its own right. There is much here for the hill walker and a lot of ground to explore if you study your map. And as for the photographer, well if he comes here with camera and tripod he will be in for a photo fest as the views down to Borrowdale and beyond to the Scafells are unbelievable and not just in good weather. You can get some really atmospheric shots from up here on days when brooding clouds scud across the sky and Glaramara and Causey Pike look unforgiving.

Let's not fool ourselves, we are not talking of great altitude and mammoth proportions. At 1,203 feet this is one of the lower Lake District heights but probably has far more charm than many a higher summit in the district. And it has something for everyone. The experienced walker can ascend from Keswick and make a decent circuit by descending the summit ridge east to go down to the farm at Brundholme and return to town by way of the old railway track that is now a lovely walk and cycleway. The elderly can potter up here from the high car park and re-live their hill walking days all over again and the very young can romp around the friendly paths on the fell. My own children enjoyed many an ascent to Latrigg whilst very young and still do even though they are much older now. It's such a friendly place. You could never climb Latrigg and be depressed or grumpy on the top. You may start out that way but once you find yourself on that high grassy promenade overlooking the north of Lakeland your spirits will soon be raised. Maybe doctors should be giving it out on prescription to our multitudes of depressed residents!

Nothing can spoil a day here. Even the new wheelchair access path will soon blend in and become a familiar part of the landscape because this is an all accommodating fell that welcomes everyone and everything and doesn't have a vicious bone in its body. I'll tell you one of the many stories I have from Latrigg and you'll see what I mean about the fun side of the hill.

A few of us set off one damp 5 November to climb to the summit from Keswick with a few flasks, a large sky rocket and a grand picnic. Our intention was quite simply to reach the top and admire the fireworks over the Lakes. Nothing too dramatic, just an early winter night time hill walk with a purpose of sorts.

We used the regular route we were all familiar with up Spooney Green Lane and took our time to get to the summit. It was dark when we set out and cold too. But the cold soon gave way to a warm mist and drizzle and by the time we reached the top most inches, our clear evening had vanished in a swirl of clag and there was no view except the glare of head torches bouncing back at us off white mist.

Now, after all the preparation, all the time spent to get there and all the anticipation, I would have expected us to be a bit miffed about the whole thing going sour. In fact we had a great evening. Out came the butties and flask, someone had brought a bottle of wine too and about ten minutes later a family of five appeared out of the mist. They had had the same idea as us and the kids were desperate to see the fireworks. We never did see any of them. We heard them alright, but that was all. I have to say it was still one of the best nights I have ever spent on a Lakeland hillside. Our parties joined up and soon we had a good sized picnic going. Stories were swapped and we found we had a few mutual friends. It was a great evening and we descended to Keswick together in high spirits.

That's Latrigg for you! It's often called 'the cub of Skiddaw' but don't you let it hear you say that. There's a fierce independence here and its separate summit status is well deserved. Latrigg is part of the Keswick skyline and is well known to all local people and visitors alike. As Wainwright so correctly says, "it is to the town as Loughrigg is to Ambleside and Helm Crag is to Grasmere". I would imagine all Lakeland fell walkers have a soft spot for it and if you have never done more than 'bag' its summit from the Gale Road car park then go and give it a bit more time.

My favourite route is the one I mentioned before with an ascent up Spooney Green Lane, but I always go to the car park at the end of the Gale Road before climbing to the summit for no other reason than I like to climb up the back of the fell to get the full impact of the view opening up before me. Then descend down the east ridge to reach the cart track and return to Keswick via the old railway.

The only drawback here is the summit itself – a lovely grassy promenade up in the sky. You will be tempted to linger and you won't be able to help yourself. It's that view. You can't seem to pull yourself away from it. Wainwright was right. This is a heavenly summit, small but perfectly formed and just the sort of place to be idle on a still spring or early summer evening as dusk gathers.

As to whether you'll have it to yourself or not, I can't say. 'I ha' ma doots' as the Scots would say, but if you really want to be alone there go early on a summer's morning just after first light and watch the sun rise over the Helvellyn range; you'll be amazed at how dramatic this can be.

I have returned here often. I will go back again and again and like Wainwright I will continue to hope that there will be heavenly summits like these when we pass into the next world and enter the real Heaven. That is if I am lucky enough to get there!

I hope what has gone before will whet your appetite a little for the pages ahead. I have been both traditional and unconventional in my approach to my Lakeland days but I have always been left with a deep sense of awe at what I have achieved. I hope the following chapters impart some of that magic I have enjoyed to you.

II

LOST LAKELAND

The hustle and bustle of modern twenty first century British life has well and truly arrived in the English Lakeland. The likes of Samuel Taylor Coleridge, William Wordsworth and even, in more recent times, Alfred Wainwright, would struggle to recognise the land they once knew and loved. The roads see ever increasing traffic and the congestion in towns such as Keswick and Ambleside on a summer Saturday afternoon has to be experienced to be believed. Tourism is firmly established as a top money spinner in the region and visitors flock to the area in large numbers, summer and winter alike.

And the same applies to the hills themselves. Paths are suffering from ever worsening erosion and even finding a parking place at the foot of your chosen hill at weekends can be problematic if you don't arrive early.

Being alone amongst them can seem almost like a form of 'Paradise Lost' as you gaze behind you down a popular path at the long winding snake of people on their way up or jostle for position at a summit cairn at lunchtime. I have fled in horror on more than one occasion from the summit of Scafell Pike to get away from the thronging mass and the noise that went with it.

However, I am painting a very bleak picture here and maybe things are not as bad as I am making them out to be. Certainly, if you are selective and careful in your approach to your Lakeland days you can have peace and quiet amongst the fells and experience a little of what the early pioneers and the Lakeland poets experienced. There are plenty of places throughout Lakeland where people are still a rarity even in the warmer months and some of the hidden valleys make great and crowd free routes of ascent to the tops. With a bit of careful thinking you can seek out places you really didn't know existed and once you start down this road one thing leads to another and it becomes a habit. In the chapters that follow I will try and guide you on your way a little and tell of some of the wonderful days I have had in such areas.

I am hoping to make you scratch your head, dig out your maps, look up that top you've seen many times and wondered what it was and then go out and climb it. It will bring a whole new dimension to your exploration of the area and will take you into areas of 'Lost Lakeland' you won't be able to believe you haven't ferreted out before.

And it's an addictive pastime. Once you begin you will spend your fell days looking at ridges, valleys and odd bumps that could be summits and trying to work out firstly what they are and then, if you haven't been there before, how you fit them into a fell day and decent route.

Those long winter nights suddenly won't seem long enough as you pore away at your maps, often with magnifying glass in hand to enlarge the landscape even more, and frantically scribble down your findings with a view to putting them into practice on the more pleasant summer evenings.

I hope I inspire you and if I do nothing else, I expect I will make you pause and consider and perhaps think...I've never been there before!

A Few Forgotten Fells

I always thought I knew the Lake District and its fells pretty well. Name the hill and I would probably be able to tell you the best way up it and usually the worst as well! I was, however, bowled over by a recent question from a friend I had not seen in some time asking me about a route up Iron Crag. This sent me scrambling for my maps in a frantic fashion – was it possible there was something I had missed?

Well, yes and no really. I have to admit that Iron Crag (it's also known as Ennerdale Fell) was a name unfamiliar to me, but when I located it I found I had certainly been near it before and traversed its flanks, but had I been to its summit? I couldn't say with honesty that I had. And if I've got you pondering and reaching for your Wainwright's *Pictorial Guides*, don't bother – he never put it in! The best it gets is the briefest of mentions (unnamed) in the ridge route between Caw Fell and Crag Fell in *The Western Fells* (volume seven). And yet this is a good sized fell (2,110 feet) with a distinct top.

And the fact it is missed by a lot of the guidebooks is the reason it has become what I shall call, for want of a better phrase, 'Lost Lakeland'. There are others that fall into this category too, but more of that later. What of Iron Crag? Well, this grand and craggy fell is situated in a great spot at the head of Ennerdale on the southern side overlooking the wild and beautiful valley of Silvercove Beck.

Not to be outdone by my questioner I set off and half expected a boring day on a dull top. But what a surprise awaited me! The summit of Iron Crag is remote and little visited by walkers but is well worth the effort needed to get you there.

I first went just after the clocks went back so the days were short and to be fair, I didn't leave the car park under Bowness Knott until after mid-morning. It was a glorious day and Ennerdale Water looked superb with hardly a ripple on the lake. The walk along it towards Gillerthwaite was breathtaking and I dawdled and daydreamed as I ambled along. I had a rough plan of attack and my eye was on the long northerly ridge that rose from the head of Ennerdale Water to reach the high ground between Haycock and Caw Fell. I had never climbed this before and as I crossed the river on the wide bridge after the lake had ended, I paused to admire the view in all directions as the fells and the water sparkled in the late autumn sunshine.

The ridge proved to be all I had expected and more, a steep steady climb through a wilderness of heather and rock with Deep Gill on one side and the awesome wild landscape of Silvercove Beck on the other. It was one of those ridges you hope never ends; but it did and I climbed onto the deserted summit of Caw Fell and dropped down off it north westerly to climb steeply up to the independent summit of Iron Crag or Ennerdale Fell if you prefer. Now a word of warning if you intend to follow my footsteps. Cross to the east side of the wall at the col before you ascend the mountain as the cairn is on that side and the wall on top is high and has barbed wire and is tough to get over to the top.

It was most certainly worth it. A great plateau of desolation spread out all around me in the magnificent glory of the already lowering sun. The sea, Scotland, the Wasdale Fells – the view was magnificent and I had it all to myself. I had done a bit of research before the climb and asked one or two people who might know, and along with a good look at my map I reckoned a return to the lake shore could be made by choosing a hazard free spot further along the ridge and descending the northern slopes of the fell back to Ennerdale Water. But what if further walls were as high as the one on the summit? The sun was beginning to glow red as it headed for the horizon – there would be no time to turn back if I got it wrong. My other idea had been to continue west along the descending ridge and cross Crag Fell and drop to the head of the lake returning back to the car park on the footpath around the top of the water. Not enough time for that and anyway, I had had a great day. I returned the way I had come, back over Caw Fell. I lost the light half way down the ridge but enough remained to let me get back to the lake head. The walk back along it by head torch light watching the moon climb over the fells was bewitching. A superb day on a fell I had never really known existed or at least never knew had a name.

It got me to thinking about this whole concept of 'Lost Lakeland'. There were probably many other mountains like Iron Crag, missed out and unloved by the general hill going public. There would be many reasons for this, location, remoteness and so on; but it has to be said that when Wainwright missed them out of his pictorial guidebooks they tended to fade into fell walking obscurity for all time.

I am sure if you sat and pondered for a while, or opened up your maps, you would come up with a few yourself. It comes as a surprise when you think you have climbed all of the Lake District fells to discover there are still a few left you may have missed. And I have to say it is a refreshing discovery – I found it very exciting to reach a Lakeland summit I had not been on before and it took me back to my early days in the area when all the summits reached where first ascents for me. Time has not jaded these hills, and I still climb them with eager anticipation every day I set out amongst them, but oh the joy to find a new way up a new mountain in an area I have spent so many years exploring.

With all the above in mind I have outlined below a few other suggestions that you may have missed on your Lakeland explorations and hope they give you a few surprising days as they have me over the years.

Great How is a very interesting little top. It served as a face saver for me and my family when my kids were very young and the weather was too savage to risk high open fells. Situated at the north end of Thirlmere and only 1,100 feet high, Great How is covered in woodland and many people must have driven past it hundreds of times on their journeys between Grasmere and Keswick. It is a little gem and deserves more attention than it gets. Before the new access laws, a permissive path was the only route to the top and to be fair, it still provides the only tangle free means of an ascent. I suggest leaving the car at the parking area near the dam at Thirlmere Head and walking back over the dam wall to climb the permissive path south above the water until it curls back on itself and goes north steeply and ruggedly to the great summit where there is a surprisingly good view despite the numerous trees. Use the permissive paths to return down the east side of the hill at the edge of the tree line and come back to your car along the road past the camp site. Follow the route on your map and you'll see what I mean. It's not a long way but provides a great half day on another hill belonging to your newly discovered vision of a 'Lost Lakeland'.

It would be remiss if I left out rugged old Caw. To those who ignore Wainwright's *Outlying Fells* book (the unofficial eighth book in the series) this will be a real eye opener. Caw is a real mountain shaped mountain, and it is rugged and remote to boot. An ascent from Seathewaite in Dunnerdale will never fail to please. The fell is all access land now but the best way up is still via the green lane that climbs south west from the village and then via the mine track that leaves it on the left about a mile or so along it. When you reach the mines a faint path climbs southerly all the way to the lonely trig point on the top. You can make a circuit by returning over Pikes and Green Pikes to pick up an old track that zigzags down the fellside from a gate in the wall a few hundred metres north east of the summit of Green Pikes or you can return the way you came. You'll wonder why you've never been here before.

THE LITTLEDALE HORSESHOE

One of the best ridge walks to be had in the north of the Lake District (and perhaps ranking the highest in the whole of the National Park) is one that a lot of people will not have undertaken and which could have them scratching their heads for a few moments.

The Littledale Horseshoe falls very defiantly into the theme running through these pages – namely a lost part of Lakeland amidst more familiar areas that you may have walked over or through many times before.

As I said in the first chapter we are not going to find a region where no one goes at all and which no one is aware of, what we are looking for is something that makes you rub your chin and ponder as you try to place it. It may be that the surrounds are well populated and equally well known but once you have identified your 'ideal people free spot' you can use it for ascent to the tops, descent from them or for simple exploration. Or if it is a top itself it can be incorporated into a day with more familiar ground.

Littledale is a little frequented valley and in its upper reaches it is wild and remote. A half decent path follows Scope Beck on the west side (it's actually an old mine road) and high above the valley on the eastern flank another path heads towards Littledale Crags. Both of these wonderful routes into this hidden dale become much more indistinct once above the dam, the old reservoir and the lower waterfalls. Once in the remote upper reaches the walker finds himself in as wild a landscape as he will encounter anywhere in the Lakes. Walking here is a delight, but perhaps a bit intimidating on a first visit or a day of lowering clouds and brooding skies. I hope that I dropped enough hints in that introduction to point you in the right direction, but if you still find yourself puzzling over the name. Let me put you out of your misery.

Littledale is the valley enclosed by the north west ridges of Robinson and Hindscarth with delightful old Newlands Church and Little Town at its entrance. Littledale Edge runs along the skyline at its head and the enclosing walls are Hindscarth's airy Scope End Ridge (well known to generations of walkers) and Robinson's High Snab Bank Ridge (perhaps not so popular, but deserving of much more recognition than it gets).

Nestling within this exciting skyline is the deserted wilderness of Littledale and a circuit of both ridges in either direction (although I favour climbing Robinson first and I'll tell you why later) makes a superb Lakeland outing – high and airy with two decent sized summits and far fewer crowds than you get if you do the more usual Newlands Round nearby.

At seven miles it's not an overly long route – you could easily fit it into a longish morning or afternoon, but my advice would be to make a day of it, linger on the ridges, soak in the view from the tops and take home memories (and lots of photos!) of one of the classic Lakeland horseshoes that you may not have considered before.

This is not a 'step by step how to do it piece' – I'll let you have fun with your maps and guidebooks for that.

I'd also like to take a look at this great horseshoe and some of the fun I have had doing it over the years. Robinson is a strange name for a fell, one of the strangest in the Lakes and it's one of the only tops to be named after a person – the gentleman in question here being one Richard Robinson who owned a lot of the land in this area several hundred years ago. The top became known as Robinson's Fell which became abbreviated to Robinson.

Incidentally, the other notable summit to be bear a person's name is Symonds' Knott on the Scafell range which was named after the twentieth century Vicar and guidebook writer Henry Herbert Symonds whose book *Walking in The Lake District* is an out and out classic and whose granddaughter still lives in the Cockermouth area of the north Lakes.

It has to be said that having climbed Robinson from every direction (and in almost all conditions – it's one of those fells with a high starting point at Newland's Hause and is great for the days when you only have an hour or two to spare) I have to vote the ascent to the summit up the narrow ridge of High Snab Bank as the best of all.

If you start your day at the car park south of Little Town near Chapel Bridge you'll be able to enjoy our horseshoe with a minimum of road walking and also have the whole route laid out before you as you pass Newlands Church. I always pop into this wonderful church anyway if passing, but to stand near it and trace the two ridges we are looking at today and gaze up Littledale is a great start to any Lakeland outing. All is laid bare and the country to be conquered unfolds at your feet (well, more ahead and above you) and no red blooded walker will be able to linger long without the urge to continue becoming overwhelming.

This is a walk for a good day. The paths are distinct throughout and it would be easy to follow in mist, but that would be missing the whole point. Come here for the views, for the breathtaking scenery and the awesome photogenic ridges that drop off so dramatically on both sides and make you look like a true mountain explorer in your photographs!

Wainwright considered High Snab Bank Ridge to be one of the best things that Newlands had to offer a walker which is rare praise indeed from a man who thought this area to be one of his favourite Lakeland destinations. And when you think of the competition all around, you realise just how good that makes it.

Access to the ridge is gained by heading up Littledale for a short way past the buildings of High Snab and Low High Snab and a steep pull is required up a grassy slope to gain the crest. But once there, a superb path meanders along the ridge top giving great views into Littledale below left and to the Newlands Hause road to your right.

This is a route that offers a bit of everything and often catches people out because, after a minor bump at the end of the flatter section of the ridge, the shoulder of Robinson rears up steeply and you find yourself having to negotiate four rocky steps. It's 'use your hands' time and it is proper scrambling but not sustained.

However, for those not used to such terrain, some of the moves can feel exposed and a bit off balance.

Don't let it put you off, wait for dry weather, take your time and you'll be fine. My wife and I arrived at this point when we climbed the ridge one frozen January day and found these rocky steps coated in ice. Having climbed them before we just went on without much thought and what transpired was an epic climb of very scary proportions which saw us fairly cragfast in several places. We hadn't expected the conditions and had no crampons and axes with us nor a rope and to say it was dodgy is an understatement. I obviously lived to tell the tale but there were on or two moments!

Above the crags the path takes you steeply to Robinson's summit which can be a bit confusing on a first visit in mist. From here a sharp descent next to the ridge fence in an easterly direction will take you to Littledale Edge with stunning views up to Honister Pass and Fleetwith Pike.

Littledale Edge is one of those great Lakeland places we all just rush through on our way somewhere else. And yet the views down Littledale and over to Honister are awe inspiring and I always think this would be an ideal spot for a wild camp or a long lunch stop on a warm day.

The old route used to climb the steep rise ahead next to the fence and go left along Hindscarth summit ridge once at the top. There is a traversing path now that heads north west from the col and works a direct route up the mountain flank to arrive almost at the summit. Of course you could (especially if there were lots of people around on a sunny day) make a quick escape into Littledale and enjoy the solitude it offers and the exciting positions it presents you with. But it's there for another day if you simply want to carry on.

I like Hindscarth. Admittedly the main cairn is a bit back from everything, but go north along the ridge to the large wind shelter and ancient cairn that marks the top of Scope End Ridge and tell me you are not impressed by the view from here. I once spent a pleasant half hour feeding a mouse in this cairn with Mars Bar pieces. He appeared from under rocks and kept coming back, getting quite tame, until the chocolate was gone and then he vanished. A fair weather friend!

My other abiding memory of this top is arriving here at the end of the best night time walk I have ever done. We traversed the Newlands Round from Catbells on a night of full moon, snow covered tops and temperatures below minus five. We enjoyed it so much (it was a full on mountaineering expedition to be fair) that we couldn't bear to come down so we simply turned back at Hindscarth and went round again in reverse!

Described by Wainwright as "an enchanting track along a heathery crest", Scope End Ridge does not disappoint. I have left it for the descent for two reasons. One is you get the most awesome views of Skiddaw and the Coledale Hills as you walk down this superb ridge and the other is, that if you leave it until day's end, most of the walkers doing the Newlands Round will have vanished as it is nearly always used as the way up on to the ridge and therefore busier in the morning – another point to consider when planning a Lakeland route and hoping to have solitude.

Scope End is a ridge with it all – breathtaking panoramas, steep drops, nice rocky bits to scramble down and amazing photo opportunities.

I haven't really touched on Littledale the valley so far in this chapter but it is well worth exploring and not many do. In its depths you will find lovely waterfalls and magnificent mountain scenery all around. I suspect, like others, I first used Littledale as a fast descent route to the valley if weather closed in – at least that's how I remember discovering it. It deserves better.

You could use it for a remote ascent route to Littledale Edge in your never ending quest for more of 'Lost Lakeland' and then come down either Scope End Ridge or High Snab Bank Ridge giving you two separate routes and two wonderful days.

Or you could simply use it as sunny day or Bank Holiday destination, a place to explore alone or in good company as the mood takes you and a wonderful place to linger and picnic.

Whatever your reason for going there don't leave it too long – more and more of these remoter valleys are becoming popular. The famous Lake District writer Molly Lefebure knows Littledale well and told me recently that she has noticed an increase in the number of people who now head up it. And if the rumours I hear of the old gold mine at Scope End being re-opened as a tourist attraction are true then the area will come under more pressure than ever.

If ever there was a time to go to Littledale it's now – but maybe I have given too much away already!

Exploring the Ridges of Keskadale

When Lakeland's most famous guidebook writer, Alfred Wainwright, suggested the name of 'Keskadale Edge' for the north eastern ridge of lowly Knott Rigg, you would have expected the path along it to have broadened significantly as hundreds followed in his footsteps and the route gained the inevitable notoriety anything he sang the praises of achieved. And yet, even today, this great ridge that runs straight as an arrow from the valley floor to the summit of Knott Rigg is little known and the route up and down it unfrequented.

Keskadale is one of those lovely sounding places that you feel you ought to know as soon as it is mentioned. You rack your brains, you try desperately to locate it in your mind and yet it just won't slot into place.

Keskadale is the valley that houses the narrow fell road that runs between Braithwaite and Buttermere – the one that climbs to Newlands Hause and then drops so dramatically down the other side with great views of the Red Pike Ridge across Buttermere.

All visitors to Lakeland will have driven along it at one time or another, few will have stopped except for a wander up to the waterfall of Moss Force from Newlands Hause or to use the parking area here as a high level starting point for an ascent of Robinson.

And yet this area has lots to offer the walker and one of its main attractions has to be the solitude. The ridges of Knott Rigg and Ard Crags on the Dales' northern side see little in the way of foot traffic and you only have to stand on the summit of Knott Rigg and gaze up at the Causey Pike ridge above you to realise just how many people can get out on the hills around here. An endless stream of walkers can be watched proceeding along Scar Crags in the direction of Sail on an average Saturday while you may very well be in complete isolation on your lower ground.

Don't let lack of altitude put you off coming here though, the two summits of Ard Crags (1,860 feet) and Knott Rigg (1,790 feet) may not top the magical 2,000 feet mark, but give a delightful fell day that can be made as short or as long as the fancy takes you – and the views are breathtaking. It is the panorama to the north that bewitches on a lovely clear day. Walk down Keskadale Edge in the afternoon with the sun to your left and slightly behind and tell me you don't take dozens of photos of the Vale of Keswick, Catbells and the Newlands Round, but most of all of the Skiddaw Massif and Blencathra, both of which are stunning when viewed from this point.

I first came here on a freezing winter's day when the blizzards cleared in the late afternoon and we were looking for something to do for a few short hours before dark. The Lakes were well and truly in the grips of winter but the road was still passable and we had driven, somewhat precariously, to Newlands Hause and parked up. We were, not surprisingly, the only ones there and three of us set off for a quick bash up and down Robinson to salvage something out of what would otherwise be a wasted trip. The snow was not too thick considering how much had fallen and it was slushy low down as we climbed. A bitter wind had picked up and we were well wrapped up with full winter gear as well as ice axes and crampons which proved useless until we got onto the top few hundred feet or so. People tell me that they think the way up Robinson from Newlands Hause is a boring ascent but it seemed far from it on that particular day. Above Moss Force on Buttermere Moss, it was boggy under the snow and as dusk was coming early due to the low early January clouds, we set a fast pace and were soon sweating profusely under all the gear. It was, however, one of those days when you froze as soon as you took something off, so we persevered. Wainwright challenges all who climb Robinson this way in his *North Western Fells* to try and do in under an hour. We did him proud, but only by five minutes!

A quick descent saw us back at Newlands Hause with a bit of daylight to spare so, being younger and much more reckless, we decided to climb Knott Rigg as well. It was a top none of us had been up before and we covered the mile to the top in good time along the lovely ridge.

With it still not dark we took a vote and agreed to push on and bag Ard Crags (I told you we were a bit reckless!) but no matter how fast we went we had no chance of beating the darkness to this top.

Still, two new tops at the end of a winter's day wasn't bad, and as darkness came the sky cleared, the temperature dropped, and we enjoyed a winter's night descent back over Knott Rigg. It was great and we probably took far too long over it, pausing often to point out mountain silhouettes and star constellations. The drive back down off the Hause was a bit of an adventure as the road had begun to freeze, but we made it back to Braithwaite in one piece – eventually!

I expect most people's experience of Keskadale is similar, perhaps not with the adverse conditions, but certainly in that they use it (or certainly Newlands Hause at the head of it) as a high starting point for a quick ascent when time has run out to do much else. It's a shame as this 'passed over area' has much to offer.

I think there are two 'classic' routes to be had here, both of which give good and satisfying days. Both are a little unusual and both involve a bit of road walking at day's end (or beginning) to link the end with the start. One is long and the other shorter, but if you are looking to explore Keskadale give them both a go.

The shorter, which I will call 'The Ill Gill Horseshoe', winds a delightful way around the ridges enclosing the little known Ill Gill and takes in both the aforementioned Keskadale Edge and the stunning summit ridge of Ard Crags. If you park at the old quarry at the end of Rigg Beck near the junction with the Little Town Road, it is as good a starting point as any. From here a superb one and a half miles will see you climbing steeply up the eastern side of Ard Crags and over the rocks of Aikin Knott (which was the alternative name a lot of old timers knew Ard Crags by). There is a good path and this is a wonderful way to ascend any Lakeland mountain. The summit ridge is one many a higher mountain would be proud of with steep drops down either side to little known Ill Gill on the left and Sail Beck on the right. The steep wall of Scar Crags and the Causey Pike Ridge gives an impressive look to the whole thing and photos taken of you walking along here will be dramatic. A further mile on a good path will take you in a gentle curve around the head of Ill Gill and bring you to the top of Knott Rigg where you will no doubt come across others who have made the ascent from Newlands Hause.

Don't worry too much as most will go back the same way! But not you – your way lies eastwards along the narrow path and ups and downs of the delightful Keskadale Edge. It will stagger you as you walk this way that this is not a more popular route with a much wider path, but be grateful for small mercies and enjoy the solitude and most of all those views. At the farm at the bottom you will be well satisfied with your day and the road walking back to the quarry will detract little from your feeling of achievement. It's a simple route but well worth having a go at on a clear day.

If you want something meatier, how about undertaking the mighty Keskadale Horseshoe? This involves parking at Chapel Bridge below Little Town and walking past Newlands Church to climb the ridge of High Snab Bank (you'll remember this from the last chapter on Littledale) and scramble up past Robinson Crags to reach the summit of Robinson in around three miles. It's one of the classic ascents of the fell and a great way to start your day. From here Newlands Hause is about one and a half miles north west and the descent is very pleasant. Once reached, you cross the Hause and use the 'motorist's path' for the mile up Knott Rigg and continue along the good path for another mile to Ard Crags. From Ard Crags summit the descent to Rigg Beck and the old quarry is another one and half miles and a quiet lane will take you back to Chapel Bridge in a little under three quarters of a mile. That gives you a round of nine miles which is surprising, as when you look at the circuit from Keskadale itself, it looks much longer. It's a nice route with great views throughout and a very unusual one not undertaken in full by many.

The next time your regular walking companion complains you are always going back to the same places, tell him you will take him to Keskadale and watch the look of puzzlement come over his face as he tries to work out where it is. At the end of either of the above routes he will have a look of contentment on his face and nod his head in approval at the completion of both an unusual and entertaining day in the Lakes.

Two Hidden Valleys

As I have said in the previous few chapters, it's very hard to think of anywhere in the Lakes where you can get away from people almost totally and this applies even more so in the popular valleys and approach routes – especially the dramatic and winding ones. Here you will not only find the throng of the regular walkers heading towards cols and distant tops, but also numerous day visitors who will include picnickers, non-walkers and the merely curious amongst their numbers. The situation becomes worse if there is a car park near the valley entrance and a surfaced path giving access to it.

There are, however, a few valleys where you can often go all day and see no one else and surprisingly these also remain relatively unknown to the majority of Lakeland fell lovers.

Here's an interesting question: what's three miles long, usually deserted, climbs to a very high level col on real mountaineering terrain and is enclosed by a stunning ridge on the west and a 3,000 feet summit on the east? The final bit should narrow it down a little, but I'll bet you'd still struggle to place the area quickly.

The valley I am talking about here is Southerndale, the winding steep sided trench that runs roughly north/south between the Ullock Pike to Carl Side Ridge on one side and the steep slopes of Skiddaw on the other. And while all the fells that surround it get plenty of attention almost every day of the week, you'll be hard pushed to find a walker who will tell you he has made a trip up Southerndale for any reason. This is a real shame as this is not only one of Lakeland's 'lost' valleys, but is also a dramatic and haunting place to visit.

I read somewhere quite recently that only a very tiny portion of our wild terrain is more than five miles from a motor road, and in the same review the author explored the theme that there were very few places left in our overcrowded land where those who wanted to could feel truly alone. I am not suggesting for one moment that Southerndale is as remote as that or even a long distance from civilisation, but it feels that way. There's a 'lost world and hidden valley' sense to it and the view along it if you walk southerly gives you a picture of Carl Side Col that makes the ascent look awesome and certainly far more difficult that it really turns out to be.

However, I am getting ahead of myself here – let's go back in time a bit. I first 'discovered' Southerndale, if that is the right word to use, on a day of March gales many years ago. Our intention had been to start at the lay-by near the Ravenstone Hotel on the A591 Keswick to Carlisle road and climb along The Edge, over Ullock Pike, Longside and Carl Side to traverse Skiddaw descending to the North Col with a return being made via Broad End and a descent to join the good track from Dash Falls arriving on the road again near Peter House to return over field paths to pick up the very end of the Ullock Pike Ridge.

I suppose, with the weather being what it was, it was destined never to happen. Severe gales were forecast for the Lakeland tops but it was one of those unusual days when the winds were not accompanied by torrential rain and scudding clouds. This was a real spring day in every sense of the word. Blue skies and fluffy white clouds in abundance, but oh the wind and the wind chill it brought with it! It came from the east and there were warnings of some structural damage at lower levels but the four of us had driven some distance to spend the day together, and although we were normally respectful of high winds (they were the only real thing that bothered us in those days), we were seduced by the blue skies and hint of spring and the better days to come. As we donned our boots by the roadside, we were optimistic and decided to give it a go as we had made the effort to get there.

Despite the sun it was bitter as we worked a troubled way along The Edge. It was nearly impossible to stand on Ullock Pike and we took a real battering along the rest of the ridge and especially at Carl Side Col. There were dark mutterings about 'turning back' but no one wanted to be the first to suggest it, so on we went. Climbing Skiddaw gave some protection from the easterly gusts but once we joined the summit ridge we knew it was all over. It was impossible to stand, and although we could clearly see the trig point ahead, there was no way we were going to get to it. The wind was quite literally a living thing and its strength was frightening. It hit the ridge with a mighty 'boom', ebbed back and then came again. Retreat was the only option and we rushed back down to Carl Side Col, and as so often happens on days of bad weather, it seems to get worse once you have either made the summit or decided to give it up. This day was no exception and we had to sit on the ground close together at the col to avoid being blown over.

It felt a bit surreal being in full winter gear under a blue sky but with the wind chill it was around minus ten and storm force blasts hit the hillside. We looked at Ullock Pike Ridge and no one seemed keen to give it a go. The wind had definitely picked up and it was strong enough to blow you off a crest such as that. Our options were limited and after a huddled conference with a well protected map we looked north into Southerndale and without further ado we headed over the edge of Carl Side Col and down very steep and trackless ground.

The way was over real ankle breaking terrain and it took us half an hour and a drop of a few hundred feet to reach protection from the wind, but as we picked up the upper reaches of Southerndale

Beck we stopped for a bit of lunch and to take stock of our surroundings.

I was impressed and enchanted and have been every time I have been back to this valley since. The head of Southerndale was a vast amphitheatre of breathtaking mountain country. Carl Side Col loomed dark and brooding up above us with Skiddaw higher again, but best of all was the Ullock Pike Ridge that worked a way along the skyline traversing what looked like a rocky crest. It looked unclimbable from the valley floor but I have since taken several routes up the rock and scree here and it is not as formidable as it appears from below. Many times since that day I have sat in the valley and watched a procession of walkers going along Longside Edge far above impervious to my presence down below.

And only twice since then have I met other people in Southerndale. One was a farmer with two dogs looking for sheep and once, about two years ago, I met a small party of teenagers who were planning to camp wild there for the night. I was gutted. From that first day it had remained my little sanctuary and to think of others spending the night there seemed to me wrong somehow (selfish, I know!).

The attraction for me has to be the solitude and the remoteness that you experience and the thrill you get when you know that the usual hustle and bustle of the Lakeland hills is going on all around you and yet here you are, sat in the middle of it all without another soul near you.

It can be very grim here on a day of low light and clag and the rocks and cliffs of The Edge can seem threatening and intimidating. Early morning in winter with a frost on the ground can be pretty, but to see the valley at its best you need a summer's day with the sun riding high in the sky. There are some winter days when I expect the valley floor gets no sunshine at all. You'd never go into raptures about an exquisite beauty here but what you see is what you get – all laid out before you, and there is a sense of solitude and isolation that is more reminiscent of a northern Scottish Glen than a Lakeland Dale.

Southerndale is a great way to get down from the Skiddaw area on bad days such as the one I described, but it can equally be used as an ascent route to do a circuit of either the Ullock Pike Ridge or the Skiddaw Massif – you just have to make sure you park in the right place to minimise the road walking at the end or the beginning of the day.

There is a good track or 'sledgate' that rises up a fair part of the valley before the trackless upper reaches. These sledgates were (and are) wide grassy trods which were formed by the passage of sledges when the stone for the fells was brought down for wall and barn construction, and they remain today as a valuable way to help you through rough ground.

There is a bridge near the valley entrance that gets you over the beck. And not far above this, on the end of the Ullock Pike Ridge, is the strange stone formation known as 'Watches'. It's a weird name and many people believe the rocks to be a druids' circle but they are in fact a natural formation.

Going back to the bridge, it can be used to link both sides of the high ground surrounding the valley in an unusual horseshoe that not many people know. It follows the skyline around Southerndale and gives intimate views down into it. You climb Ullock Pike and proceed along The Edge from near the Ravenstone Hotel in the usual manner and then proceed via Carl Side Col to climb Skiddaw.

Now here's the clever bit. To return, you can either descend to the north col and work a rough and tumble way down the side valley of Barkbethdale or continue to Broad End and zigzag down the west slopes back to trend left near the base to the start of Southerndale. Or for the really adventurous who like a bit of mountaineering in their fell days, a superb and tough descent can be made from inbetween Skiddaw summit and the south top following the ill defined north west ridge around Randal Crag and so on down. It takes a bit of scouting around to get yourself established on the upper sections of this route, but as you descend the going gets easier and the path develops and is easier to follow.

You'll get a great day out and it will give you an insight into the character of Southerndale, now you know it exists! Wainwright called it "quiet and unfrequented" and little has changed in the decades since he wrote about it. If you want a real slice of a Lakeland lost valley take an outing along Southerndale and experience a quietness you had forgotten existed and discover an area you were a bit hazy about too!

And so to our second valley – and it has just as much in the way of interesting features and remote terrain as the one we have already looked at.

I was asked recently if any areas of Lakeland could be mistaken for a Scottish Glen. I suppose there could have been several answers (including Southerndale of course), but for me there was only one I could give. It had to be the hidden and little known valley of Shoulthwaite Gill that runs in a southerly line between the High Seat to Bleaberry Fell Ridge to the west and the forested uplands belonging to United Utilities that cover Raven Crag (the one above Thirlmere Dam), Castle Crag fort monument and the little visited summit of The Benn in the east.

This secretive valley and water course is an outstanding example of truly 'Lost Lakeland' and the days when you encounter another walker here could be counted on one hand. This area of Lakeland is very reminiscent of Scotland. The Shoulthwaite Valley is a long narrowing one with woodland on one side and magnificent rock scenery on the other. The high retaining walls tower above you as you walk along it and the path meandering roughly down the western side could easily be mistaken for a stalker's path in the Highlands.

Shoulthwaite (the correct pronunciation is 'Shoolthet') is right amongst the heart of all things Lakeland and hidden deep amongst the central fells, separated from Borrowdale only by the ridge of high ground that runs from Bleaberry Fell to Armboth Fell. Shoulthwaite Gill is where the water from the eastern side of High Seat and the aforementioned Bleaberry Fell drains from the higher ground. There are numerous water courses running down the fellsides here, but the major one that joins Shoulthwaite Gill below Castle Crag Hill fort (also known as Shoulthwaite Hill Fort) is Mere Gill. This is an awesome ravine and gives rise to the Scottish comparison again, particularly as you are getting towards the upper narrowing reaches of the main gill when you reach this point. Anyway, Shoulthwaite Gill continues tumbling southwards down rocky steps through wild ground to empty into Naddle Beck which feeds the River Greta.

By now I am sure you will have placed the valley or looked it up on your map but I am willing to bet that many of you will not have been there. It's a place I have come to often over the years – a haunting area, wild and wonderful. On a day of spring sunshine it is quite enchanting and in winter frost it is breathtaking, but come here on a brooding day of low clouds or as darkness falls on a winter night with the mist gathering, and you will really know what it means to have shivers run up your spine. It was such a day that saw me visit this area initially.

Well, to be fair, it wasn't quite like that when I set out alone to climb the Gill one early February day many years ago when there was just the hint of a long awaited spring in the mild air. The long winter nights have always been a time for me to catch up on my reading and I usually have a long list of climbing or walking books I intend to work my way through. And it was amongst these I first saw Shoulthwaite mentioned.

I was intrigued. I thought I knew most valleys and gills in Lakeland so in desperation I turned (as always!) to Wainwright.

"Shoulthwaite Gill, quite near the main road, yet hidden from it, should find a place in every walkers itinerary" he wrote. I spread out the maps and began to form a plan. "The valley", Wainwright continued, "forms a narrow ravine between craggy walls". That was enough for me.

With a good forecast for the weekend I decided to set off and explore this secret valley for myself. As always the weathermen were not to be trusted.

I decided to follow a 'Wainwright route' up High Seat in the central fells that used Shoulthwaite, and later on Mere Gill, to climb to the summit. I loved the place as soon as I saw it. I have often taken people there since and no one has ever been disappointed. I climbed alone stopping often, intending to come back from High Seat over the marshy ridge to reach Bleaberry Fell and then work a rough passage back down to the gill. The weather held until I had climbed beside the awesome lower ravine of Mere Gill and followed its boggy upper reaches to the lonely summit of High Seat.

I had started late and didn't reach this point until well after three in the afternoon. There was noone else around (there very rarely is on this top) and I watched fascinated as the lovely February day deteriorated before my eyes and black clouds rolled along Borrowdale and dropped on to the tops. The temperature fell rapidly and it began to sleet. It was getting late and the days were still short, so I decided to retrace my steps back the way I had come. It was easier said than done.

In the clag and gathering gloom I struggled to find the upper reaches of Mere Gill with the result that, by the time I got below the cloud line and back to the path besides Shoulthwaite Gill, it was getting dark fast. Out came the head torch and although the sleet had stopped, it was still freezing. I hurried along the gill but it was an uneasy passage. Shoulthwaite Gill after dark on your own can be a spooky place.

I very rarely get scared but I didn't like it there that night! I kept glancing over my shoulder and hurrying as best as I could on the rough terrain and was glad to cross the stile in the wall beyond where the old weir used to be. It may have been the towering fellsides above and the darkness that was blacker than black, but to be fair I have never felt comfortable on this gill at night despite having been down it a few times since.

But daytime is a different matter. Stand at the end of the valley and look southwards on a fine spring afternoon with the sun high and behind you half right and you will be entranced.

Here is Lakeland in the raw and it simply beckons you to come and give it a go. The unclimbable looking fellsides to your right are almost frightening as you run your eye along them with the cliffs of Iron Crag looking very impressive indeed, and as you begin to settle down you can trace ways out of the main gill and up through the crags and broken ground. I have climbed many routes up these fellsides and it would be unfair to say they are easy, but they are challenging and a test of your route finding ability in difficult terrain. The main route on this side of the valley would be the classic traverse of High Seat and Bleaberry Fell (mentioned earlier) reached via Shoulthwaite Gill and Mere Gill. It's a good rugged outing and it's unlikely you'll meet many others on it. Of course, you could follow the gill all the way up to its head and continue along the forest edge rising right slightly over boggy trackless ground to pick up the right of way from Armboth (at Thirlmere) to Watendlath climbing to the boggy summit of High Tove to walk back along the ridge north returning over High Seat and Bleaberry Fell. It's probably not worth it (apart from giving you the opportunity of getting into some really wild Lakes landscapes) as it does nothing to add to the aforementioned route.

Returning to the valley head you could be forgiven for thinking the trees of Raven Crag and The Benn on the left would give no access to higher ground, but you would be wrong and United Utilities have a permissive path network here whereby you climb all the way up to the wonderful viewpoint of Raven Crag. Or you could park at the dam wall at Thirlmere and come over Raven Crag on the paths, dropping to the entrance to Shoulthwaite to pick up the valley by a bridge over the gill. You could have a good day exploring it before following the permissive route around the base of Raven Crag and back to your car again.

Most people will access Shoulthwaite from the footpath a little north of Brackenrigg Farm on the A591 near Keswick, but as well as the way described over Raven Crag you could use the permissive path that leaves the minor lane between the Keswick Road and the Thirlmere Dam and passes alongside Shoulthwaite Moss. This will bring you to the same point as coming over Raven Crag.

If you do visit Raven Crag take time to follow the signs for the Castle Crag Hillfort below it. There's not much of it left but the view from the top of it down Shoulthwaite is one of the best you will get of the valley – particularly in the morning with the sun in the east.

A way can also be worked off Castle Crag to enter the valley near Mere Gill, but to be honest it is steep and rough and a little overgrown and you need to be quite determined if you intend to do it. Best to stick to the easier ways.

Here's a quote from Wainwright to finish – "It is a black pit in storm but arrayed in bewitching colours when the dying sun lights its shattered cliffs and screes". He was talking about Wastwater when he wrote that, but apart from the sunset on the cliffs (which face east and don't get it, but sparkle in the morning instead) the words could equally apply to Shoulthwaite.

Go and have a look for yourself.

THE GLORIES OF GLACIAL GREENBURN

I hope by now I have whet your appetite for seeking out Lakeland's hidden places and have given you an insight into how to go about it.

This section looks at a little history and a very distinct area in which it is created. During the last (and most recent Ice Age) extensive ice would have covered much of present day Lakeland and only the very highest tops such as Helvellyn, Skiddaw and Scafell Pike would have poked a frosty summit above the ice line – looking for all the world like frozen islands in a world of frost. The glaciers that covered the area were (and remain elsewhere today) the most powerful of all natural erosive forces, grinding a slow and unstoppable way downwards between the tops leaving the familiar hanging lakes and valleys we see so often in mountain country and gouging out deep trenches behind them with tell tale 'scrape marks' along rock and heaps of glacial moraine.

Lots of people walk for a lifetime in the Lakes without realising that many of the valleys became what they are today as a direct result of glacial action and tracking down remnants of this can be a fascinating pastime if you know where to look. About fifteen years ago I worked with a young chap called Dave who had a deep interest in the natural world, was a keen conservationist and a member of Greenpeace and was a mine of really interesting facts and snippets of information about the great outdoors.

He came on several trips to the Lakes with me, and the days were always long as we often paused to examine such things as moss, plants, rocks and the marks left behind by receding glaciers.

I found it fascinating and it was on one of these trips I discovered the 'lost valley' of Greenburn.

Going back to Wainwright again you will find he referred to this secluded bit of the Lakes as "a valley that is unfrequented and yet deserving of attention", and he was right. The surprising thing to a lot of people, myself included, is that they will probably have walked along the southern rim of this valley on many occasions, and may even have done a horseshoe around it without even giving it a second glance. It's one of those places you tend to overlook because it is in the company of much more famous bedfellows.

And, as I discovered on my first visit, it is a valley that we ignore at great loss to ourselves. Greenburn is a lovely bit of hidden Lakeland. It's full of interest and glacial history, a great way into the heart of a decent group of fells with a few unusual routes from the valley floor to boot, and is very secluded and lacking in other people.

So, let's get the geography sorted out first and place this little bit of 'Lost Lakeland'.

The Greenburn Valley is a long, rising and (certainly in its lower reaches) narrow valley that ascends through wild, rough and lonely country next to a lovely brook (Green Burn Beck), past waterfalls, to open out at the head of the beck into a vast amphitheatre of space, an enormous bowl of wilderness country where you will stand and feel very small indeed.

This is known as Greenburn Bottom and there are plenty of moraine lumps in the vicinity indicating the ancient presence of glaciers. Dave reckoned that there had been a cold glacial lake in the location long ago and subsequent investigations I did in books seemed to bear this out. Certainly it is a fascinating place on a bright day, but an eerie area when the mist is down and swirling around this vast bowl. It's possible to walk right across Greenburn Bottom but it can be swampy in places. And after that a steep and rugged uphill pull will bring you right out of the Greenburn Valley close to the old boundary fence that runs along the wide marshy ridge between Calf Crag and Steel Fell. It's not the best way to exit this fascinating place, but it makes for what I call 'a semi-mountaineering route' and certainly takes the walker into territory that others never see.

To follow the good path on the right side of Greenburn up the valley is an enchanting experience with the terrain becoming gradually wilder as the ascent progresses and the skyline of mountains all around takes on different prospects as they are viewed from below and then looking back down the valley.

If I tell you that Greenburn is surrounded by a superb horseshoe walk that in itself is not that well known as a 'round' and that the southern side enclosing mountain wall is the lovely ridge running from Helm Crag over Gibson Knott to Calf Crag and that the entrance to the valley is guarded by the south east ridge of Steel Fell (as well as the northern wall of Helm Crag), you will know just where I am talking about I hope.

You will have no doubt looked down into the wild lands below you on your hill walks in this region but not really considered a trip into them. Well, don't be put off further, the next time you get a day of nice clear weather get off early to nab one of the few parking spaces for a car on the roadside near Gill Foot Farm and give yourself plenty of time to head up into Greenburn and explore. The best way to exit the valley after you have walked along its length is by cutting left as you reach Greenburn Bottom (over stepping stones that help you across the marshy head of Greenburn). And then simply follow the path, which is distinct enough not to lose, as it zigzags up to join the ridge line between Gibson Knott and Calf Crag at a cairn. And from there you have a couple of choices – both of which are very appealing. You can either go left and return along the well walked ridge to reach Helm Crag and then return to your car by following the traditional Grasmere route off Helm Crag and going left just before Goody Bridge (or earlier if you want to short cut the pretty route back towards the town) following the minor roads back, or you can turn right and go over Calf Crag to circle round the head of Greenburn Bottom and return over Steel Fell.

And for something different how about the Greenburn Horseshoe? It is one of those lesser known Lakeland rounds that is fast gaining in popularity and is a splendid outing around the Greenburn Valley with ever changing views of the surrounding fells, an enchanting high level path over some fairly remote and wild terrain, and a superb descending ridge to complete the day.

Basically it combines the two routes mentioned above with a slightly different start. It can be begun and finished at Grasmere to lengthen it somewhat, but that means a bit of road walking at the start or end of the day.

Far better to park at Gill Foot again and climb into Greenburn, crossing the neat bridge over the beck a little way along it and following the highly visible path to reach the col between Gibson Knott and Helm Crag and then climb to the top of the latter. You'll need to backtrack to the col again but once you are on the ridge, the route finding is easy all the way to Calf Crag where a little bit of map reading and careful navigating will take you on the faint path skirting Greenburn Head with good views back down the valley, to pick up a line of old fence posts and a better path that will take you all the way past a couple of wild tarns (nameless but sometimes called Steel Fell or Rough Crag Tarns) to deposit you on the summit of Steel Fell. This is an often overlooked Lakeland top and is the western guardian of the pass of Dunmail Raise. There is really only one way off Steel Fell worth considering and that is the south east ridge. Fortunately it forms part of our route and the superb path down it is followed, with an odd diversion to skirt crags, all the way back to the entrance to the Greenburn Valley.

Once you have done this route you will wonder why it has taken you so long to enjoy it and why Greenburn has been overlooked on your Lakeland fell outings. Well probably because it's quite concealed really and the company it keeps is very hallowed. Yet it has a dignity and uniqueness all of its own which makes it a venue you will return to often. When you apply the above criteria of being hidden and having famous surroundings, it will probably make you dig out your maps because other such places will start to spring to mind and you start wondering what else you might have been missing.

Just like soul searching, there's nothing wrong with a bit of map searching – you never know where it leads!

THE NEGLECTED LAKE

To finish this chapter we should look at the lakes themselves. After all they are nearly all very popular with overfull car parks and people milling around everywhere. Surely there must be one or two of them that fit into the category of a 'Lost Lakeland'?

Well yes there are and I will concentrate on just one of them here and that is Brotherswater near Patterdale. It is tiny compared to say, nearby Ullswater but it has a character and charm all of its own and really is a Lakeland's lake in miniature with all the bits and pieces you would expect from the largest of them. And yet as it is located between the famous Kirkstone Pass and the equally famous Ullswater it is usually overlooked and ignored and best of all it is surrounded by great fells with lots of unusual ways up them which you may not have come across before.

My most poignant memory of what I often consider to be Cumbria's 'neglected lake' was perhaps not my greatest visit to its shores. It was mid-summer, raining hard and I arrived there by accident; well perhaps more by negligence – let me explain.

My intention had been to take advantage of the light mornings and walk around the Fairfield Horseshoe – I had some commitment or other in the afternoon and this has always been the way I have maximised my time on the Lakeland fells. Up early, head off a little after first light and then down to the car park as a lot of people are only just arriving. It's not for everyone, but I love those hours and you nearly always have the tops to yourself.

So leaving Ambleside as the town lay sleeping, I headed for Rydal over the fields via Low Sweden Bridge and Rydal Park. It was already raining and it got steadily worse as I climbed the steep ascent to the top of Nab Scar and headed off on the good path around what must be one of the best of the Lakeland horseshoe walks. Somewhere between Nab Scar and Heron Pike the clag rolled down the ridge and it didn't lift for the rest of the day. With it came a wind, a nasty savage thing that drove the relentless rain hard into my face. So much for summer; I was in full winter gear by the time I dragged myself on to the summit of Fairfield and got into one of the low wind shelters to cheat the wind. Despite the hat and gloves I was wearing I was cold and soon began shivering. The visibility was almost zero in the swirling cloud and the rain was relentless. The forecast of the previous evening had warned ominously of heavy showers and a 'freshening wind' but this was daft.

It was time to look at my options. As it was about the same distance to go back as to go on, I decided to finish the route. Bad weather has never intimidated me too much and although the summit of Fairfield can be difficult in mist I soon navigated off it and onto the good path that runs down the second part of the ridge over Hart Crag, Dove Crag and High and Low Pike.

The weather had worsened still when I arrived on Hart Crag and the rocky summit swirled in and out of the mist. The path I began to descend on didn't seem familiar to me and I felt it was dropping too much but I carried on regardless. I knew I should have been going south easterly at this point but my compass indicated north easterly. I ignored it. How could such a great path be going anywhere but around the Fairfield Horseshoe – the compass had to be wrong? A fatal error we have all made occasionally.

In recounting the story since (to many chuckles) I put it down to the weather and the soaking I had taken. There was no visibility as such otherwise I would have seen the crags of Link Cove to my left and realised what I was doing. Instead I stumbled on down and then up and over the rocky up thrust of Hartsop Above How and it was only as I descended its long curving ridge by the wall that I came out of the mist and a sorry looking Brotherswater and Hartsop appeared below me.

I looked behind at the raging storm and decided I would be wiser carrying on down to walk along Brotherswater, past the campsite and Hartsop Hall to return to Ambleside up Caiston Glen and over the Scandale Pass. It made an eleven mile day into a nineteen mile day but it seemed like a good idea at the time! I didn't see another soul on the hills all day and Brotherswater looked anything but inviting. But it's not usually like that.

If you were to go through the various lakes in Cumbria in your mind you would probably find that you had spent time on the shores of most. In fact over the years most of us have walked around all the main ones, if not in one go then over time in a series of disjointed sections often as part of a route up the fells or a way back at the end of a day spent on higher ground.

But what about Brotherswater? Situated as it is further south and higher up the valley than its more loved bigger brother Ullswater, and connected to it by the lovely Goldrill Beck, it is often passed by with a quick glance by motorists as they head to the Kirkstone Pass.

This is a shame and in many ways this pretty place has become the neglected lake of Cumbria. Most know where it is, many have passed it but not many have taken time to explore the area around it.

As a place I think it is wonderful. It's a little 'lost world' all of its own. If you camp at Sykeside Farm just above Brotherswater or use the camping barn there, you will find you can get no mobile phone signal, no radio signal and no TV signal. You are simply hemmed in by the high ground, and the views of ridges and valleys are awe inspiring to say the least. And once you get above the valley floor and look down the incredibly steep sides of some of the fells here you can see just what a gem Brotherswater is, closed in all around by tops and nestling in such a gorgeous wooded valley you'll wonder why you didn't take more notice of it before. Maybe it's a size thing. After all Ullswater is huge and so is Windermere. But then again Grasmere and Rydal Water are not that much larger so what is it that sets this place apart?

It's just one of those places that you pass and glimpse through the trees along the roadside and then carry on. And yet take my advice, give Brotherswater a chance and you won't regret it. This is a great little lake and a superb starting point for some good hill routes. I once spent a week's holiday here and didn't move the car once but we managed to climb six out of the seven days and never did the same route twice.

It's a place to come and relax, a place to walk the hills returning to this hidden valley in the evening, and a place to dream about and go back to many times afterwards.

Many of the valleys and ridges here suffer a similar fate to the lake. They are simply superb and yet as routes to the famous tops that overshadow them they are relatively unknown.

Take Dovedale, the rugged valley that cuts into the hills and which must give one of the wildest sights in Lakeland when viewed from the flatlands of Hartsop and Upper Patterdale. How many times have you used this as an approach to Dove Crag and the Fairfield Ridge? Probably not at all and yet this is a fabulous route that Wainwright hails as an "interesting and intimate approach" and "far superior" to the ascent from Ambleside.

This is a rewarding place with lots of new routes to old favourite tops that you will probably never have climbed or explored before. You really are amongst the heart of hill country here and yet get out your guidebooks or go on the internet and try to track something down about this area and you'll see what I mean about it being neglected. The centre of all things here is the Brotherswater Inn and the adjacent campsite and as a base for exploring the surroundings you couldn't do much better. Car parking is limited elsewhere except in nearby Hartsop and back towards Ullswater at Cow Bridge, but don't be put off, give the place a chance.

I read once that Brotherswater got its name from an old story of two brothers who fell through ice and drowned here on a New Year's Day many years ago after trying to walk over the lake. If it is true it is a sombre tale to go with such a lovely place.

From a hill walker's perspective there are endless days to be had here. The National Trust owns much of Brotherswater and a path goes around it, not always too close to the lakeside but a circuit can be made.

And as for the surrounding hills there are no end of combinations that can be achieved. Let me offer a few suggestions for unusual routes you may never have tried before.

The much underrated summit of Caudale Moor is usually climbed from the top of the Kirkstone Pass, but try climbing it from near the Brotherswater Inn up its broad north west ridge and you will be astounded at the dramatic aspects you get of this summit as well as the amazing views you get of Brotherswater and Patterdale far below. This has got to be one of the great unknown ridges of

Lakeland. At the top a great sweep around lonely Caudale brings you to the rambling summit and a great return can be made to Brotherswater over Hartsop Dodd and down to Hartsop. But before you leave Hartsop Dodd walk a little way west from the summit for what must be one of the scariest views in the Lake District. The fellside simply falls away at your feet here and the steep hillside drops to Brotherswater, the inn and the campsite hundreds of feet vertically below. There is a zigzag path down this monstrous drop but I have always had trouble finding the top of it. I once went straight down the fellside on a nice summer's day and I have to say it was one of the most frightening descents I have ever made down a British hill.

Then you could try a good circuit over High Hartsop Dodd and Little Hart Crag with a return over Red Screes and a descent of the other steep ridge the area has to offer, the north ridge of Middle Dodd. I'll bet there's plenty here already you'll not have done before but that's the magic of this place. You could climb Hart Crag over Hartsop Above How and carry on to Dove Crag returning back down Dovedale.

High Street is accessible from here and a lovely circuit of Gray Crag and Thornthwaite Crag makes a nice day with a walk into lovely Hartsop always being a pleasure.

I could list a lot more but space won't permit and maybe it should be left to you to go take a look yourself and discover this 'neglected lake' and its surrounds for yourself.

One things for sure, once you've been here you won't pass it by without stopping again!

III.

LAKELAND ODDITIES

There are certain things that are uniquely Lakeland and in our minds we associate them with the place all the time. These are the obvious things such as the lakes themselves with the backdrop of fells around them. We may think of Keswick and our favourite shop or pub, or many of us may conjure up images of Blencathra as we drive along the A66 on our way to yet another Lakeland adventure. It may even be a certain campsite or a car park at the start of our favourite route up Scafell Pike.

As we have already said, there are so many aspects and facets to the Lake District outdoor game that it would take a dozen volumes to list everybody's favourite and even then much would be missed out.

But there are other, sometimes obscure areas that are often connected with lesser known aspects of Lakeland life and fell walking in particular. Many of these will be something you may have heard of or even tried. At the very least you may have wondered about them and marvelled at the people who get involved in them. In this chapter I want to look at what I usually term 'Lakeland Oddities' – those strange occurrences and odd ball pastimes that, I suppose, in many cases could be linked to high mountain country anywhere but seem to have developed in the Lakes more than most places. This is probably because the Lakeland Fells are better documented than most mountainous areas of our country and also because more people probably come to Lakeland than say, Snowdonia or the Scottish mountains.

This is only a superficial explanation of course, and this quirkier side of Lakeland Fell walking has many more devotees than you might imagine.

I hope I am not painting it as some subversive sub-culture that should be avoided at all costs because it isn't! It is so much more than that and I hope in the following pages to introduce you to some areas of the Lakeland outdoor scene that may enhance your hill days or at the very least, add another facet to your enjoyment of this unique landscape.

FOOTY FAN ON THE FELLS

On a breezy May Saturday with bright sunshine and blue skies we arrived on the summit of Great Dodd after walking over from Clough Head as part of a long day route we had had planned for some time. It was a day of little sunshine despite the cloudless sky – the wind was chilly and the sun was failing to add any warmth to the proceedings – but the clear air gave us the most dramatic views we could have wished for. Later we intended to follow a complex return trip over Stybarrow Dodd and Sheffield Pike before continuing to our start point late on at Dockray. But for now other more pressing matters filled our minds.

We had left lunch until late on purpose for two reasons. One was that we wanted the summit to ourselves and secondly...well it was F.A. cup final day and being an avid Manchester United fan I couldn't bear to miss the match with old rivals Arsenal. It was a bit chilly for sitting around at that height so we tucked ourselves up inside a two man survival shelter and sat on rucksacks munching butties with a small radio on very low as we listened to the game.

Now, I expect you are throwing up your hands in horror at this point. Radios, like mobile phones, are seen as an abhorrence in the great outdoors. How could I possible condone the use of one on such a lovely view point as Great Dodd?

I don't intend to try and justify it! Like a lot of others, I have to take my hill time when and how I can get it. Work commitments, family ties and lack of babysitters often mean that I am out climbing in the most inclement weather when others have the luxury of being able to give it a miss and come back the next day.

And those days often coincide with Man Utd. match fixtures. Try as I might I can't bring myself to choose between my hill walking and scrambling and my love of football and there are days I am not proud of it. It's led to all sorts of strange happenings over the years and I work very hard not to let it interfere with anyone else's enjoyment of our magnificent hill country, but it's an addiction I can't leave alone and sometimes find impossible to work around. So hopefully you will also find something to laugh about in my tales of the smaller pleasures of life amongst the Lakeland fells.

You may find yourself surprised, as I have down the years, to learn that I am not the only one afflicted in this way. I'm not saying there are hordes of fell walkers obsessed with football results each Saturday afternoon (and sometimes on Sundays as well) but you will find it is more common than you think. And you're right, it probably has no place on the tops, but if you're doing no one any harm, not forcing noise on others and getting enjoyment out of it yourself, what damage are you really doing?

Back to Great Dodd then. Obviously the food ran out faster than the ninety minutes of the game and we quickly drained the flask. It was warm with the sun beating down on the shelter and it seemed like we had the main Helvellyn ridge to ourselves. How wrong we were!

Bracing myself for the cold wind beyond our warm cocoon I nipped outside for a pee and was staggered to see four others around the summit cairn (which is not really on the summit here). We hadn't heard them arrive and they had made no noise whilst there. I strained my ears to hear the radio in case it was too loud, but it was barely audible over the wind. Relieved, I smiled but decided against answering nature's call when one of them was a woman.

Then I got the surprise of my life. "What's the score?" one of the men asked, "please don't tell me Arsenal are winning? Oh, and if it's all the same to you could you turn it up a bit so we can hear the last fifteen minutes!" Of course I obliged! There wasn't enough room for six of us in the two man shelter so as they had lots of grub, we moved outside to them. The only down side was that Man Utd. lost that day!

On another more recent day – a couple of Easters ago actually, I was doing a lovely snowy round of Newlands. It was full winter conditions and although great fun and superb mountaineering weather, it was bitterly cold. Now my other ploy for getting up to date scores if a match and a hill day coincide is by using my mobile phone and connecting to the sports pages that are updated every two minutes or so. It keeps me happy and when you have two football mad kids with you as well, it is an essential bit of kit.

As we descended Dale Head on route to Hindscarth, Man Utd. had just put a second goal past Liverpool. Carefully watching the descent, I let the kids see it on the mobile and they cheered.

A lone walker coming the other way stopped and instead of passing the time of day with chat of weather and snow he asked anxiously, "is that the United game you're checking on?" I confirmed it was and he asked tentatively, "are they winning?" Result – one happy pilgrim sent on his way rejoicing!

We have tried so many ways of keeping up to date with the score over the years that I have forgotten a lot of them. The number of walkmans, tiny radios and the like that have bitten the dust in Lakeland storms are too numerous to list. The favourite trick of putting an earpiece in to avoid sound and annoying others fails if the rain comes down fast as they seem to get sodden and crackle and fizzle before dying forever. And if the wind is blowing it whistles behind them and into your ear and you simply can't hear so you have to put a hood up or hat on. What an idiot I have looked over the years on hot days dressed like this and all for the love of a team that don't always win (but don't lose that often either – I had to add that bit!).

And then there was the episode of the shower radio that we were bought by a dotty aunt one Christmas. Why anyone needed a radio in the shower seemed beyond us – I never spend enough time in there to get any benefit from it. It was guaranteed as waterproof so an idea hatched in my mind. Maybe it would fair better than previous 'prototypes' had on the hills on match days.

I tucked it into my rucksack at the top with an ear piece and we set off to climb Bowfell and Esk Pike from Great Langdale on a day of indifferent December weather.

The biggest problem was that I put it on top of the rucksack liner assuming that if it could survive a shower it would be safe enough.

Wrong, wrong, wrong!

The rain started near the top of The Band and by the summit of Bowfell it was torrential. At three I turned my radio on and tried to tune it in – it was totally dead. It may survive a typical English shower but Lakeland's heavy rain beat it in no time at all.

Then there are the problems of getting reception for both phones and radios. Hills and these items don't go together unless you stay high. Many are the routes that have been modified to accommodate an over tense game as the signal has vanished as we descended. This usually means going up again and staying up there until either victory is assured or the game is over!

FANCY A BIT OF GILL DIPPING?

The first time I came across anyone taking a dip in a Lakeland gill was so long ago that I was still in my late teens. We had come to the Lakes after some years climbing the Snowdonian Mountains and a swim in a high level tarn in a hanging valley was a fairly traditional end to a summer's day there.

In the Lakes it was something we had never seen and we began to think that walkers and climbers this far north were a little more reserved (or a bit softer!) than the tougher bred Welsh lads who seemed happy enough to go skinny dipping in all seasons.

We were brought down to earth with a bang (a very pleasant one it was too!) one sticky August afternoon when we came down Sour Milk Gill into Easdale after a day on the Langdale summits. We were headed for Grasmere for the night but as the path rounded a corner we came to a deep pool on the gill with a little waterfall dropping into it – and splashing merrily away were two very good looking blonde women in their twenties. One was in a t-shirt and her underwear but the other obviously didn't want to wet her upper clothes and was 'taking the waters' topless.

For two young lads such as us it was a great end to what had been a superb day. The girls we found out later that evening when we met them in the pub were Swedish (what else would they have been?) and our enjoyment of the moment was only marred when a very fat and hairy gentlemen joined the party in his shorts and growled menacingly at us!

Taking a dip at day's end in a Lakeland beck is a great way to cap off a nice summer's outing. Now I know you are going to tell me that we don't get the summers for it anymore and certainly a lot of years we don't. But if you go prepared, take your swimwear with you and have somewhere in mind, you never know, the weather may just play ball for you and you can dive into the icy waters (they never seem to get warm) and enjoy a great freshen up before you descend to the valley. I am not advocating that you follow the example of the two well known Grasmere lads Timothy Tyson and Colin Dodgson who made it their business to bathe in every Lake District tarn winter or summer alike (they dipped in 463 of them in total and Timothy was seventy six when he did the last one!) but I feel they do epitomise the very essence of the adventure.

And adventure it is. Those beckoning green waters that appear so inviting when your chosen beck drops into a grassy hollow are always deeper than they look and can be very cold, but once you get into the water you will be like a kid again and there will be no getting you out. Tarns are a different proposition as they are often muddy and full of leg grabbing weed, but becks and gills tumble into the most glorious of pools with crystal clear water that simply begs you to jump into it.

If you really fancy a dip in a tarn (and this feature is most certainly not about that practice) may I suggest that one of the best for this is Sprinkling Tarn under the cliffs of Great End. Here you have deep water next to rocks so you can have a really good play around and there is enough depth there to do some real swimming and not just splashing from side to side.

However, let's get back to 'gill dipping' as I have dubbed the pastime. There are one or two drawbacks and words of caution that need mentioning before you put you Speedos under your Ron Hill's next time you are hill bound, but mostly these are common sense.

Obviously you need the weather! The main months for this pastime tend to be from late May to mid-September – May can be cold, September can be delightful if the month falls sunny. The three main summer months are often a bit of a lottery for the majority of years in England, but rest assured you will get a few decent days of sunshine at some point during them, so go prepared.

Swimming gear and a towel (you really need one to get yourself dry and get any grit off your body before putting clothes back on or the walk down can be uncomfortable) don't take up much space or add much weight to a rucksack.

And apart from a lack of recklessness, that is about all you will need. During the summer it is worth packing the gear whatever the forecast. Mountain weather is fickle and a dull start can turn into a glorious day later on despite what the weatherman says. And don't worry too much about the fact it may have been cold the week preceding your proposed dip. Most swimming points in our gills are in hollows were the sun only penetrates for a part of the day anyway, so no matter how hot it is, this, combined with the ever running mountain water that tumbles down, always keeps the pools a bit on the chilly side. Don't be put off though. Once you get in and get used to it it beats a dozen showers!

Make sure you check for any nasty obstructions such as a branch that has come down the beck from above that could snag your feet and have a good look around above for any dead sheep. They have a habit of expiring and falling into gills and I once camped (in Scotland not the Lakes it has to be said) at a lovely burn pool where we drank and cooked with the water tumbling down the rocks above. We thought the brackish taste was due to the peat until we almost stood in the rotting sheep wedged at the edge of the water fall above our camp site the next morning as we set off!

And don't dive in – check your depth first. Take a bit of time and it will be an accident free and pleasurable way to spend a later afternoon in summer.

Finally, make sure there is not nasty vertical dropping waterfall below you as well. In an unguarded moment you could easily go over.

My preference is always to gill dip on the way down from the fells. You are tired and dirty and it is just the ticket to put you right again. If you try it on the way up you will linger too long and waste your hill day. Going down to the pub is always beckoning so you will not over stay your welcome.

The only real bank side hazards are midges, mosquitoes and flies that can attack you once you get out. They seem to have a penchant for beck water, and even though they are not a regular problem they can be a positive nuisance on a still and muggy afternoon in late July or August.

Although I have done the skinny dipping thing a few times in my life it is not a practice I recommend. There are simply too many others on our fells now and you really wouldn't want to scare your fellow walkers would you?

One of the best descriptions I have ever read of Lakeland gill dipping is in Hunter Davies's classic book *A Walk around the Lakes* when he describes a wonderful swim he had with his children after an ascent of Scafell Pike on a hot summer's day. He chose that wonderful deep green pool just above Stockley Bridge which would be high on my target list when in this area. He described the subsequent fun as "the most pleasurable swim I've ever had in my life". And that just about sums it up. Get it right, find a good spot, and hey presto you are in for a real treat. It's not an exact science but, with a bit of trial and error, you will soon find a few places of your own to give it a go. You have to make sure your descents from the high places follow routes where you are most likely to find suitable pools – and that obviously means gills!

These bathing paradises can be found just about everywhere in Lakeland and I have listed some of my favourite areas and pools below. It only takes a little bit of extra work to include a gill as part of your descent at day's end.

For instance even an unusual round such as a scramble up Halls Fell Ridge on Blencathra starting at Threlkeld could include a dip at day's end if you descended northerly over Foul Crag and across the strangest Wainwright top of all, Mungrisdale Common. A visit to this barren moor is a rarity for most and a rough descent south west will bring you to Glenderatarra Beck where you will find a few decent dipping spots before you return to Threlkeld via the beck and the base of the mountain.

That shows you that even a diverse route can include the pleasure of a swim if you plan it right. There are numerous well known gills and becks that you will no doubt have walked down (and up) many times and once you get your mind working, the ideas will simply flow. Keep your eyes open even on winter days, as what you come across can be stored up in the mind for next summer. Explore some of the more remote gills and you will be surprised what turns up – at the very least you will get into places where there is often no path and some very rough walking which sees little foot traffic.

One final word of caution though, do make sure you know just what you are climbing up or down and don't be tempted to go into dangerous looking terrain in some quiet watercourse. Keep it safe and simple, stick to what you can see is safe and let people know where you intend to be at day's end and you will soon discover a new side to your hill days and will wonder, as you relax in nature's very own bathroom and feel the sweat of the day wash away, why it has taken you so long to take part in this rewarding game.

My all-time favourite place to have a dip at day's end is where Greenup Gill and Langstrath Beck meet at a 'T' junction just above Stonethwaite in Borrowdale. This is dramatic country anyway with great peaks all around and plenty of fell day opportunities to bring you here at day's end. This is a really nice and wide pool where you will find others join you once they see you having fun.

Others such as Stockley Bridge at Seathwaite have already been mentioned but try the little visited Greenburn Valley between Helm

Crag and Steel Fell and you will find some nice pools. Also, and great for a day on the Coledale Hills, a descent down Stoneycroft Gill under Outerside and Barrow can be quite an eye opener.

The list is endless. Wherever there is running water coming down a valley you will find pools – the choice of the destination and the wonderful adventures to be had there are ultimately down to you.

A Crash Course in Aircraft Location

It must be about twelve years since I last went out deliberately to find aircraft wreckage on the Lakeland fells. I was reminded of those days recently when, quite by chance, I came across a bit of scattered metal whilst doing a longish route out of Eskdale.

My wife and I had left Brotherikeld Farm at the foot of the Hardknott Pass, walked to Esk Hause, continued to Scafell Pike and then climbed Scafell by way of Mickledore and Foxes Tarn. We had planned to return via Slight Side and as we had made good time we took a more leisurely pace back from this often neglected top and as is our wont at such times, we started to meander.

I believe in filling every minute of every hill day and I have always hated getting back early to my car so when it looks likely to happen, I deviate and explore places I haven't been to before. And it was while doing this that we came across some wreckage. I knew what it was straight away as I had been involved in finding such sites over a decade ago which I'll tell you more about later. But on this particular Sunday afternoon the mist had started to come in thickly and we didn't stay too long but just scouted around a bit and found what wreckage we could before we made our way back.

The next day I rang my old friend Paul who knows about these things and an hour later I had an answer. What we had found was actually the wreckage of two aircraft on Slight Side and Paul thought they were Hawker Hurricanes that crashed into the mountain side after getting into low cloud during a flying exercise over the Lakes on 12 August 1941. The pilots of both aircraft had been killed and he even gave me their names and ranks. There should have been a memorial cairn nearby too he informed me – but I had failed to spot it as the weather deteriorated and we had made our way off the mountain.

I first met Paul on Ullscarf one late winter's afternoon in thick clag and he was well and truly lost. Paul was no fell walker but he had a passion for tracking down crashed aircraft (most of which are located in mountain terrain) and he frequently got into trouble in his pursuit. We hit it off straight away and over the years that followed he got me to navigate him to crash sites all over the Lakes, Snowdonia and the Peak District. He was setting up a small museum with photos from the sites and background to each aircraft with pictures of the crew and details of what happened.

I found it very fascinating as I like navigating in difficult terrain and there was something thrilling about finding a wreck in the middle of nowhere after a careful search.

Paul was new to Lakeland and its crash sites and I found myself much in demand. Sometimes, if his friends, wife and relatives came for the day it could be quite a party I ended up shepherding over the fells and remember, a lot of these had little, if any, hill experience (or mountain dress sense either!). Paul was what you would call obsessive – once the date was set nothing deterred him or made him change his mind.

Many were the times we spent long hours in some hidden side valley of a remote gill looking for pieces of wreckage and I probably learnt more in those years about guiding people in hill country than I ever did before or have since. Paul wanted to write a book but he never did, although his little museum got off the ground for a short while. He lives near Dartmoor now and we still keep in touch.

The first site he asked me to take him to was the one we all know, the one on Great Carrs of the Hercules Bomber that crashed in 1944. I had been there many times before but never realised (although Wainwright indicates it in the Great Carrs section of his fourth book *The Southern Fells*) that the better part of the wreckage lies down in the Greenburn Valley under Swirl How and includes a good section of the fuselage. We scrambled down from Broad Slack between Great Carrs and Swirl How and took photos. It marked the start of a three year period of such expeditions.

We searched for a spitfire on Scafell Pike in vain in an early November snowstorm but later found out it was on Ill Crag. For various reasons we didn't get back that way until the following April and we never found it. I did speak to a man some years later whilst camping in Great Langdale who claimed to have located it and told me where. I went back alone but still failed to spot it.

And I suppose that is part of the fun of the whole thing. Sometimes you win and sometimes you don't, but the real thrill is in the search, the wild country you get into and the fascination of being able to piece together what had happened all those years ago once you are safely back down.

Lakeland is a great place to undertake a venture of this sort. Leaving Great Carrs aside there are a fair number of crash sites on the fells and probably many more waiting to be re-discovered. Most date from the Second World War in the days before sophisticated navigational aids when fog and low cloud could spell disaster for pilots who had received minimum training.

Some people have told me they find the whole practice macabre and that such places are in fact war graves and should be left alone. But many have cairns and plaques nearby in memory of the brave young men who lost their lives at that point and, although the toll was sometimes horrific from a single crash, it is a harmless pastime and keeps the memory of these lads alive a bit longer if you are prepared to take the time to search out the events that led to the disaster.

There is little left at most sites except scattered metal, perhaps an odd identifiable bits of plexi-glass amongst the rocks. It's hardly surprising really when you think that most have laid out on the fells, exposed to the elements, for upwards of sixty years and let's be fair, an aircraft crashing at a hundred miles an hour plus into a rugged hillside is not going to leave a great deal intact anyway.

Not all the planes that crashed were as old as those mentioned above. Paul got wind of a Piper Cherokee dating from 1966 that was located near Esk Hause and a date was set for a visit. We failed completely first time as the group leader (me!) was far more interested in scrambling up gullies on Great End, it being a dry and sunny day at the end of a similar month. But a return visit a week later (again in sunshine) reaped a reward. By this time Paul had done his homework and knew all about the aircraft. There wasn't a great deal to see when we found it, but apparently the Piper had flown from Milfield in Northumberland on 17 September 1966 flying to Carlisle and then south along Borrowdale. Here the starboard wing struck a big rock near Esk Hause and was torn off causing the remains of the aircraft to hit the ground killing both the pilot and his passenger.

All these details are there for the finding if you know where to look and the internet is a great place to start. I have listed a few of the crash sites I know of or have heard of below but you will have to search the areas unless you can track down an exact grid reference and these are often non-existent.

I recommend someone like my mate Paul to help you out but failing that, a few sites to look for always helps. You will need to be extremely confident at navigating and not afraid of trackless terrain in remote locations often far from any paths. You'll also require a good dose of luck, a camera and a nose for finding these things, something which develops the more you do it. Once in a general area it becomes obvious where a plane might have hit and a search has to be made. Remember you are often only looking for fragments of engine or fuselage which may be between rocks or in gullies but many times you will find a lot of the wreckage has been piled up by previous visitors making it easy to spot.

And remember to treat these places with respect. Most of the time people died in these crashes. Take nothing away, leave it as you found it and use your photos as records.

Paul always wanted to find a piece of the pilot's steering column or the armour plating that surrounded his seat (in war-time aircraft) but he never did. Apparently they were the rarest pieces of all and seldom left at sites. Pause for a while and reflect on what took place here and then give thanks that you, at least, have yet another day on our hills to enjoy. It's sobering and it makes you appreciate your hill days a little bit more than you might think.

SOME CRASH SITES TO TRY AND FIND

Esk Hause – Piper Cherokee
Iron Crag – Sabre Mark 6
Eel Crag – Halifax Mark 11
Scafell – Hurricane Mark 1
Caw Fell – Oxford Mark 1
Ponsonby Fell – Canberra

And remember, not all the sites will be on summits. Try to find what direction the flight came from and make an assessment from that information and better still, try to get a grid reference if one exists. I have purposely not put the ones I know against the sites above so as not to make it too easy and turn these places into picnic spots for all and sundry. And at the risk of stressing points that are probably obvious to all, do make sure you are very proficient with map and compass before heading off into wild remote terrain well away from paths and other humans!

CATCH ME IF YOU CAN!

We all know the scenario very well if we spend anytime amongst the Lakeland fells. Out alone and loving it, you glance over your shoulder at what you thought was an empty fell side only to discover another walker behind you appearing as a coloured dot far below. A little further up you risk another glance and the 'dot' has grown to a distinguishable figure and is gaining fast. You are already sweating and puffing away and could do with drink and a short stop but no one likes to overtaken on the climb to the summit, do they? You struggle on and find an extra spurt of speed giving it five minutes before confidently sneaking another furtive glance to the rear. And there he is, looming much larger now and probably only a few hundred metres behind you. And what's even worse, he doesn't appear to even be warm let alone close to hyperventilating.

It's always hard to know what to do in these situations – maybe age has finally come knocking on your door even if you are refusing to go and answer it! If so, it may be better to stop on the pretext of getting a drink or with some face saving ploy like checking the map. You can give a cheery, "nice day for it", as he storms past and then resume at a more sedate pace.

At least until the next competitor in this unofficial and highly competitive Lakeland sport steps up to the mark and comes into view behind!

Oh, yes, make no mistake about it, human racing on mountains is a tried and tested Lake District tradition in the same vein as

Cumberland wrestling or gurning. And no matter how much you resolve to have no part in such a childish thing that has no place on the fells, just wait until the next time a party appears to your rear as you plod up Helvellyn or Glaramara and then tell me afterwards that you didn't increase your pace to stay ahead and get to the top first.

The summit is the finishing line, of course, at least on the uphill sections. But going downhill at day's end it can be the car park or the pub or whatever you choose. And though you may dread it happening on the steep up bits, we are all guilty of participating on the down parts too.

You spy a group in the distance ahead and with 'Chariots of Fire' playing in your brain you make it your business to beat them to... well, to wherever it is you need to beat them to. The aim is to pass them. And once they spot you coming they will be out to stop you doing it. And the race will be on again!

I used to think that solo walkers were the worst for this and I put it down to them wanting to give themselves a little something to do to take the place of the lack of a companion and conversation. But over the years, I have had to revise that viewpoint. Groups can also be very competitive either collectively or if the leader is of that ilk. To give an example, I recently took my kids up the Long Stile Ridge of High Street on a sunny winter's day. It was the best day for weeks so the car park at Mardale Head was packed and the fells heaving with people. If you take your kids into the hills regularly you will know two things. Firstly they quickly get much faster than you and secondly they can say the most outrageous things to other people but not realise they are being offensive! The consequences can range from hilarious to exhausting!

We were going well up Rough Crag, but as usual mum and dad were trailing behind the youngsters who seemed almost to float from rock to rock and never appeared short of breath. There was a party ahead who had left the car park at a brisk pace with a tall upright no-nonsense sort of ex-military chap in the lead. I had chatted with them for a few moments and they were over from Gateshead for the day and intended to circle around High Street, Mardale Ill Bell and Harter Fell. It was a great day for it and after casting a disapproving look at my youngsters who were fairly noisy, the leader took his party off hillward.

With two kids we take forever to get ready but once we get going we can cover a fair bit of ground briskly. The party of Geordies were becoming rather spread out ahead as the leader's pace was obviously far too fast for the stragglers at the back. He began to glance anxiously over his shoulder at us and urge his back few on. You may think it's annoying being overtaken by adults, but believe me, people go potty about kids hurtling past them. I don't understand why as most kids over ten are very fit and fast but try telling that to grown ups!

Anyway, we continued to gain on them with the usual cheeky comments from my two such as "if that's as fast as you can go isn't it time you gave this up Dad?", and other encouraging quips in a similar vein. There was obviously a rebellion in the party ahead as they suddenly stopped, downed rucksacks and got out drinks and cameras. It was a gorgeous day and by the time we reached them there was much 'fell spotting' and past day recollections going on. The leader sat alone on a rock with his rucksack firmly in place looking daggers at us.

And this is where a child's innocence comes in. As we passed we called hello to them and then my daughter said to the leader, "it's no good sitting there all day in the sun, you know, you'll never get around like that".

I have never seen a man almost explode before, but I did that day. He went red from the neck up in seconds and we quickly moved on.

But it was too late, the damage was done. We heard him behind us snatching Mars Bars from open mouths and ordering kit be stuffed back in rucksacks. The hapless party were bullied to their feet and the race was well and truly on.

Now we were as guilty as anyone else of fanning the flames at this point. You see, in human racing you may not take part intentionally, but once you pass someone there is no way that you want to be passed by them again.

The Long Stile Ridge is steep and rough but we did ourselves proud that day. The kids pushed out at the front as always and we panted behind them casting odd glances below. The party had split again and was now four separate groups. The leader was alone and way beyond the others pushing hard to get up to us. He nearly did it too, but we reached the level ground of the High Street plateau first and put on an extra burst of speed to get to the top.

We had won!

And just to make the matter worse we plonked ourselves down next to a good high bit of wall with some rocks for sitting on close to the trig point. It was sheltered from the wind and we tucked into lunch. The leader arrived, glared at us and went to mope at the trig and wait for his divided party to arrive. "That must be the place Dave had planned for dinner," one of the ladies said casting a glance at us snug from the wind as she passed, "he won't be happy about that!"

It's pointless and it can get some people very worked up but it's also great fun and something young and old take part in whether they mean to or not. Some do it subconsciously, others make it a part of their day, be they big parties, two people together or solo walkers. It is a game with no rules and no governing body and yet it must have more active competitors than a lot of organised sports ever will.

The results can be hilarious. Parties can leap frog each other a dozen times on a day route and some will get themselves incredibly worked up over the whole thing. I like to be quite remote on Lakeland hills and keep well away from crowds, but let me spot a challenger looking to steal my thunder and I will take up the gauntlet the same as anyone else.

Let's put it all into some sort of perspective and keep it real though. We do this for fun. And I am sure the majority of people don't take it seriously, but I have to admit, and I'd lay money on most people agreeing, it's a pretty smug feeling to stay in front and beat an advancing party off. Or better still to come from behind yourself and work your way along a line of walkers ahead of you passing each with a knowing nod and a slightly sympathetic smile that tells them you know that their faster days are probably now behind them!

Summit of a Mystery

On a breezy but bright day in early summer some years ago I approached the final pull up Skiddaw in the northern lakes with a little relief. It was mid-week and as far as I could see I had the mountain to myself, a rare treat indeed!

Leaving Little Man as a treat for the way back, I hurried up the final rough path to the summit ridge drooling at the thought of the view and already reaching for my camera. It was one of those days for taking photos like you see in all the best guidebooks.

As I pulled up onto the south summit the strangest thing occurred: from nowhere a bank of cloud rolled up from Bassenthwaite Lake and obscured everything. One moment I was wind blown and squinting at the sun and the very next I was shivering in a grey damp fog with no view but the damp stones at my feet.

Pulling on a fleece I headed along the ridge for the summit. I did indeed have it to myself, but as I huddled shivering in one of the wind shelters trying to drink coffee, it was far from the utopian scene I had envisaged. I gave it half an hour and when it didn't clear I headed back down. Twenty minutes later I was beginning the climb up Little Man when the sun came out again; I looked back and there was Skiddaw awash in sunlight. I checked the time, there was no rush to get down and it was too good an opportunity to miss. Turning around I headed up the steep slope to the top for a second time.

I made it to within a hundred metres of the trig point before the same thing happened again. In came the clag and off went the view; on went the fleece, out came the flask and I gave it another half an hour. But it didn't clear. I wrote the day off and headed down. Half way there I looked back to see the summit in sun again...but I'd had enough for one day.

Now this and several other instances, which I am sure many who frequent Lakeland hill country and read these lines will be familiar with, have lead me to believe over the years that in some past life I must have offended one of the weather gods and he cursed me for all eternity!

I appreciate that the Lake District gets more than its fair share of rain and mist, I can live with that, but this goes beyond simple meteorological data in any format. It's just not possible to have it happen to you as regularly as it has happened to me over the years and it not to be connected to some strange karmic incident relating to your past!

Another well remembered incident went as follows. This time it was winter and the destination was Helvellyn via a wintery ascent of Striding Edge with a return down Swirral Edge. The sun was out and the sky blue when we left Glenridding and it looked like it was going to be a great day.

Striding Edge was a dream. Blue skies, enough frozen snow and ice to make it a real mountaineering expedition and a clarity in the air that made photography easy. Down the bad step and up the final pull to the summit we went, crampons crunching as they bit into the white stuff. We didn't even make the plateau before the clag rolled over the top in a slow motion waterfall that engulfed us. We tramped cold and despondent to the wall shelter and ate soggy butties with a dozen others. We headed off and took our time over the frozen accident black spot at the top of Swirral Edge and made our disgruntled way down.

Back at Red Tarn the clag lifted and the top cleared. The snow on the summit was dazzling against the blue sky. It was late in the day with darkness not more than an hour or so away but we had to go back. Up we went and it wasn't easy this time as were starting to get tired – winter mountaineering can get you like that. We got near the summit again and could see the western sky reddening as the sun started to set. This was going to be good.

The clag thought otherwise. Over the plateau it crept and was waiting for us as we came over the ice field at the top of Swirral Edge. Cold and damp we tramped back down by head torch light convinced we were in fact cursed and trying to decide what particular indiscretion in our tainted pasts was the cause of all this chaos.

To put this 'cursed and dammed' theory to the test we decided to try something smaller the next weekend and went to Catbells for a traverse of the ridge and the summit. It was a grey day but the summit was clear when we nipped into the last parking place at Hawes End. Up the ridge we went but the summit was obscured before we were half way along it. We carried on convinced it would clear. It was only a small summit after all. It didn't though and it got worse and thicker. This time our unfriendly weather god let us get down to Derwentwater again before he let the cloud lift. No one was too keen to tramp all the way back up, but a theory is a theory, and I had to give it a go. Up I went alone and sure enough down came the cloud as I neared the summit.

Now this was getting beyond a joke and I was considering options such as consulting some strange mystic or even worse, throwing my rucksack and boots in the bin! Instead I resigned myself to a life of viewless summits and was sitting at the giant cairn on the top of Scafell Pike one cold February afternoon wondering if I had enough time to climb Great Gable on my way back to Seathwaite when events conspired to convince me of my accursed condition again. It was cloudy with no view of course. Out of the gloom came a young man called Ian who was hoping to return to his car via the corridor route. Having never done it before he asked if he could come with me as I was going that way.

He was pleasant company and we chatted away as we went down. At Sty Head tarn I looked up at Great Gable summit shining in the late afternoon sunshine. Scafell Pike was of course out of clag now I had left it. Ian was keen to climb Gable having never been up it before. It was late and would mean a return in the dark and so I told Ian about my bad luck with clag and my battle with an irate weather god. Not to be put off, he smiled and shrugged his shoulders. "Don't worry about it," he said, "I always get a view from the summit if it's clear when I start. I can't remember the last time it clouded up on me on the way up."

So we shook hands on it and went for it. And to be fair to Ian we almost made it to the war memorial on the summit before a huge cloud appeared from Wasdale and dumped itself on the plateau. Down we went in the gloom but a few hundred feet below the top it cleared. Ian smiled knowingly and talked me around and we headed up again.

Suffice to say young Ian started putting distance between me and him as we headed back. He kept shaking his head in disbelief at what had happened and muttering strange words. It defies reason and I bet I am not the only one it happens to. I would also gamble on the fact that there are others reading this who, like us, choose a route for Saturday and head off in the car towards it. And invariably the mountain chosen is swathed in cloud and dark looking weather while everywhere else is bright and lovely. It is a standard joke in our house that a map is unnecessary to get to the car park at the start of a walk. We just look where the weather is the worst and head in that direction because that's where our top will be!

Not a pleasant state of affairs, not something to be proud of, and happening too often to be mere coincidence and it still remains, 'summit of a mystery'.

Number Thirty Fives

I suppose it is only fitting to finish this chapter on 'Lakeland Oddities' by taking a look at something (and someone) that is unique to the Lakes.

Wainwright's books never really succeeded in Wales or Scotland and you can only conjecture that if they did, and he had started his guidebook writing career in his twenties and not his forties, then the summits in these mountain areas would be as well known as the ones in the Lakes.

You see, one of the great differences between the Lakeland Fells and a lot of other high mountain regions is the fact that all the fells have documented routes up them and this has resulted in a path up the popular ways, even on the small ones. In Snowdonia or Scotland it's mostly the big tops that have been included in the guidebooks and the lesser heights have faded into obscurity and most have no usable ways up, except in one or two rare cases. Try climbing one of Glencoe's little summits and you'll soon see what I mean – no way up, no way through and no one interested in trying. I have often thought it might make a great (and good selling!) project to produce a guide to these tops and one of these days I might if time ever permits.

This blanket coverage of the Lakeland fells is really all down to Wainwright. He took guidebook writing to another level and nothing was missed out by him. Consequently, we have a selection of routes at all heights, for all levels of ability and, most important of all in a Cumbrian context, for all weathers. And I am sure, that like me, you have been very grateful for this over the years.

'Face saving tops' are a must in a fell walker's armoury and vital if he or she is going to make a day of it no matter what the time or year or state of the weather. The lowliest summits in the Wainwright *Pictorial Guides* have the highest numbers on the fell list on the back cover and it has become traditional amongst our walking parties to keep them up our sleeves for the really bad days and 'doing a number thirty five' (I'll explain why we dubbed them that later) is an acceptable salvage of a foul day.

It all began on one of those days when no one in the party seemed the slightest bit interested in getting out of the car. You couldn't blame them – I've started many happy mountain days, and probably just as many wet and miserable ones, from the car park at Glenridding near the head of Ullswater. It's one of those places that all Lakeland fell walkers have a store of memories relating to, a little like Seathwaite in Borrowdale which is often recalled with affection when thinking back on past Lakeland times – linked in the mind with happy fell days, setting off full of anticipation and returning content and pleased with the way the day has gone. The starting and finishing point compliment the day's walking as much as the hills themselves have. It's a strange phenomenon and not just linked to Lakeland. All mountain areas have a Glenridding and a Seathwaite.

On the particular late winter morning in question, Glenridding car park was definitely not a nice place to be. The wind howled around in violent swirling gusts that rocked the car and the rain hammered down in torrents that flooded the tarmac and turned the buildings around to a dull grey colour. It was early, the few shops were still shut and the daylight was fighting a battle with the previous night for supremacy and losing. I am sure we have all had these sorts of mornings and all felt the bitter disappointment that goes with them.

Three days earlier the fells had been snow covered and the blue skies of the daylight hours had given way to clear and frosty nights and we had put together a hastily arranged trip for a winter traverse of Striding and Swirral Edge on Helvellyn. The conditions had seemed perfect and settled and when everything had changed the day before we, had decided to take the chance and go anyway.

Our party of four had not been out together for some time and it seemed a shame to postpone things when we had all rearranged our lives a little to make the trip.

Snow or not we could still make a nice day of it. The weather man had moaned on about low pressure bringing in waves of wet, mild and windy weather the night before and the mountain forecast had warned of sixty mile an hour gales on the high tops. Fell walkers are ever the optimists and most will go take a look anyway. Most buy into the Rheinhold Messner philosophy of no matter how bad the weather looks 'it's always worth giving it a try – you never know, it might get better'.

Our car was loaded up with a variety of winter gear and we were all experienced and well used to extreme weather conditions in the Lakes and elsewhere. But this was one of those mornings when you just knew you would be wasting your time. The rain was too heavy, the wind too savage and the low clag looked menacing and uninviting.

Mentally we all gave up and resigned ourselves to numerous cups of coffee in Ambleside, but my wife was made of sterner stuff. "We've made the effort to get here," she pointed out, "we should at least have a go at something no matter how small." We looked out of the car window, shrugged and left it to her.

And it was on that long ago winter's day that the concept of 'doing a number thirty five' was born and it has stayed with us ever since and become something of a 'get out of free jail card' down the years.

We all use the Wainwright *Pictorial Guides to the Lakes* and most of us are so familiar with them we can almost name the fells in each in descending order of altitude. But it's the ones at the bottom of those lists that should always be kept up the sleeve for the atrocious days. The final one or two in each book are the ones that most of us climb to complete the ascent of them all, but which are more often than not neglected by the majority of people, and yet in their own right can give a great day out.

They are usually much lower than most of the others in these wonderful guides and, more importantly, their tops are often out of the cloud when the higher fells are covered. And being of lesser altitude they don't take such a thrashing when the weather is giving the summits of loftier heights the good news. These then became our 'number thirty fives' – the smaller hills that gave us a day out when their bigger brothers and sisters were out of bounds.

The name 'thirty fives' was used because on the day recounted above we happened to have Wainwright's first book, *The Eastern Fells*, with us and bottom of the pile here, at number thirty five, was the 1,400 feet peak of Arnison Crag. It was so foul that even this proved to be a bit tricky but at least we managed to get out on a day we had all written off.

It actually turned out to be quite a decent little route. Yes, we got a good soaking; no, it wasn't anything like what we had planned, but it took us into areas of Lakeland we had never visited before and it kept us below the cloud base so we had a view, a somewhat grey and dreary view, but a view all the same.

We walked to Patterdale, climbed up beside the wall to the summit of Arnison Crag which is a magnificent viewpoint for Ullswater, and then we simply carried on over a few minor bumps until we reached Trough Head and climbed an old rickety iron stile (still there to this day) and descended by Hag Beck through Glemara deer park and at the bottom picked up our outward route back to Patterdale.

We still went into Ambleside afterwards for coffee but it tasted so much sweeter knowing that we had got out regardless of the foul weather that had kept most people off the hills.

I have been back since and done this route in good weather when my kids were young and it was just as enjoyable. And that's the real beauty of these 'number thirty fives' they really are belting little tops that we are all guilty of neglecting because they are so far down Wainwright's lists. Be honest with yourself, if you were going for a day on the Lakeland fells you wouldn't plan it around something like Arnison Crag or even number thirty four in *The Eastern Fells*, lowly Glenridding Dodd, would you? And yet we rob ourselves of some great days on the hills by being so blinkered.

Like I said before, 'thirty fives' is a misleading name. Most of the *Pictorial Guides* don't go this high. Book two (*The Far Eastern Fells*) goes up to thirty six and has the highest number of tops, while book five (*The Northern Fells*) only goes up to twenty four and has the lowest number. As far as we are concerned the phrase 'thirty fives' will always include the last two fells from each of the seven books and we will always call them by that name after that first day in Glenridding car park!

But let us not dismiss these as insignificant fells unworthy of our attention. We have fourteen tops here, Glenridding Dodd, Arnison Crag, Hallin Fell, Troutbeck Tongue, High Rigg, Loughrigg Fell, Black Fell, Holme Fell, Mungrisedale Common, Latrigg, Rannerdale Knots, Castle Crag, Fellbarrow and Low Fell. With the exception of Mungrisedale Common (its not often I disagree with Wainwright but I can't bring myself to call this bit of flat moorland a fell!) you have a superb list of mountains with a variety of routes and distances to suit all days and tastes.

One has to be careful though. After a while we had these summits labelled as bad day routes only and this can be a mistake as all of these can provide excellent days out on good long sunny summer days too.

But it was as bad weather alternatives that our idea was born and for many years that was what we used them for – back ups for the odd days when it really was too foul or dangerous to go high.

I suppose it was really when our children came along that we began to use them for regular days out. And to be fair, they do provide a great way to introduce youngsters to the hills. The climbing is not as great as on other fells, the distances can be made quite short if you need them to be and yet you still get a huge amount of satisfaction when you get to the top of one of them. And a lot are mountains in miniature with summits better than many of the higher tops possess.

Take humble Glenridding Dodd overlooking Ullswater and overshadowed by a scary looking Sheffield Pike. Its heathery top is quite delectable as a place to visit and linger. The views are truly superb and the drops to Ullswater are dramatic. All in all a great little top that could hold its head up amongst so many of the higher fells that circle the skyline all around it and yet you will almost certainly have it to yourself.

We all know and love Loughrigg Fell but how many of us have followed the undulated ridge of High Rigg, the second of the two lowest in Wainwright's book three? A brilliant route traverses the delightful summit and long ridge from the ancient church of St Johns in the Vale until the high ground ends and a return can be made along good paths from near Smathwaite Bridge along the lower slopes of the eastern edge of the fell.

Black Fell, Holme Fell, Hallin Fell – all are worth a visit and can be made long or short (even Hallin Fell with a bit of improvisation!) to suit all tastes and all weather.

Fellbarrow and Low Fell can be linked to make a good day, and lowly Castle Crag, Wainwright's only listed fell under 1,000 feet, can be made into a long day if you are prepared to follow low paths to get to it.

Special mention needs to be given to Troutbeck Tongue which is surrounded by dramatic mountains so much higher than it and yet has so much character of its own and is so very rarely visited. At just over 1,100 feet it is not high but is remotely situated and if you don't mind a bit of rough work amongst fern and heather, a worthwhile route can be worked up the rocky rib of the south ridge with a long descent down the fell's whale back before a glorious walk out back to Troutbeck.

And finally what about Rannerdale Knotts? Here is a little gem high above Crummock Water. This is a great hill and you could really run into trouble on its rocky slopes below the summit if you rashly chose a line to descend.

I hope I have whet your appetite and given you another little something to salvage a bad day out of in Lakeland. It really is worth the effort once you have got there. You'll thank yourself for it afterwards as you drip in the café and the tourists shun you as you steam!

IV.

Peak Profiles

No book on the Lake District is complete without a look at the stars of the show themselves. It is above all the fells that bring the lover of the high places back to Lakeland season after season, year after year. And their appeal is endless. They give so much and it is all for free and there for the taking for those who know how to go about it. Their appeal goes far beyond what could ever be expected from what are, let's be honest, lumps of rock and earth.

So many of the better known fells have had volumes written about them down the years and yet many of the mid-sized ones have hardly been given any press at all. Rather than merely go over old ground again in this section, I have taken a few of the more unusual of the Lakeland hills and tried to show you what they each have to offer.

One of the dangers of the Lakes is that so many people approach it with tunnel vision and eyes always fixed to the greater heights and the better known horseshoes. Although these are classics and rightly so, so much can be enjoyed by forsaking them from time to time and heading to their smaller brothers and sisters. I hope what follows will inspire you to do just that.

Billy-no-Mates

There are certain Lakeland fells that stand apart from their immediate companions and appear to belong to no particular group at all. This is often down to location in relation to the surrounding summit groups (of which they may well form a part) and these fells are rarely visited by regular hill walkers. The paths on these 'less popular' tops can appear to range from faint to non-existent – and yet things are often not as they seem.

Seat Sandal would be such a fell. When I first climbed it about fifteen years ago during my own Wainwright bagging campaign, the track that rose from near the top of Raise Beck to the summit cairn was indistinct at best, and almost invisible in a lot of places. Over the years I have seen it develop into a better route and on a recent ascent, the first time I had been that way in four years, the path running beside the broken down wall was a good and prominent way up the fell. So, for all my misgivings about summits such as this being ignored, someone must be getting up there!

There are some Lake District tops where I have never seen another walker and Seat Sandal is one of them. But this is a mountain that has much to offer with magnificent views from the flat top and a delightfully angled south ridge that descends, with breathtaking vistas of the Vale of Grasmere, to reach the road again near the Travellers Rest Inn.

At 2,415 feet this is a good-sized fell but unfortunately it finds itself in the company of far loftier and more famous mountains such as Fairfield, St Sundays Crag, Dollywaggon Pike, Nethermost Pike and Helvellyn. Geographically it has to belong to the Fairfield group, but no one associates it with this particular collection of lofty summits, and even mighty Fairfield itself turns his back on poor old Seat Sandal and shows it an unwelcoming display of steep and rough fell side, with a tough looking path and perfectly straight old wall being the only signs that humans have ventured on the slopes that fall to Grisedale Tarn. Think of the last time you were in this area. Chances are you were on your way up Helvellyn from Dunmail Raise or had dropped off St Sunday's Crag for a spot of lunch on a wild and windswept Grisedale Tarn before deciding whether there was enough of the day left to take in Fairfield.

Grisedale Tarn (a wonderful example of a glacial hanging valley) is one of the most dramatically situated sheets of high-level water in the district, but it can be bleak on a bad day. Climbed from Patterdale or via one of the two routes from the Dunmail Raise road, it isn't usually the objective of a day's walk and is merely a point on the route or a stopping place for refreshment. Seat Sandal rises in a brooding crag to the west of the tarn. This is Gavel Crag, a tumble of scree and nasty looking rock that is possibly the fell's most imposing feature. However, few venture here, although there is a scrambly path that rises from the upper reaches of Tongue Gill and provides a short mountaineering expedition for those interested enough to seek it out.

Unfortunately, most who come to Grisedale Tarn don't even bother to work out what the fell to the west is, and those who do often decide the fleshpots of Helvellyn or the Fairfield Horseshoe are a far bigger attraction and move on to them after coffee. Only the ardent summit baggers seem to visit the cairn on Seat Sandal – and then usually only once!

But, be honest, would you ever consider setting out to make Seat Sandal the main objective of your day in the Lakeland Hills? I think most would say no, and that brings me back to my opening point about this fell being a 'Billy-No-Mates' – not included in any of the surrounding groups and shunned by the majority of visitors. So this is a clarion call on behalf of one of the gentlest and friendly 2,000 feet summits in the Lakes. I can honestly recommend a visit here and my reasons are many.

The first has got to be the wonderful summit plateau with its far reaching views. On a clear day the panorama to the west and north west is stunning with the Coniston Fells, Langdale Pikes and the Grasmoor range being framed against the distant skyline to perfection. Below, but above the Vale of Grasmere, you find yourself looking down on Helm Crag and Steel Fell (whose own southern ridge can be traced down all the way to its base) that appear as dramatic rocky prominences below. From the A591 near Grasmere, looking up towards Dunmail Raise, Steel Fell and Seat Sandal look like twins perched on either side of the pass top. The view is deceptive as apart from both having wonderful southern ridges (which are completely different in character but both give a superb route up or down their respective fells), they are totally different mountains.

Although we have said that Seat Sandal probably owes allegiance to the Fairfield group, the fell conforms to the general pattern of the Helvellyn range in showing grassy and easy slopes to the west with a steeper and craggier eastern face. Sadly big bad Helvellyn wants little to do with his nearby pretender.

Returning to the summit, it has to be said that the views of the Nethermost Pike, Dollywaggon Pike and Helvellyn to the north are disappointing as they appear as boring grassy slopes and reveal nothing of their true character, but the sight of Skiddaw, framed nicely above Thirlmere, will have you reaching for your camera. Fairfield looks brooding and unwelcoming but there is a great view of St Sunday's Crag with Grisedale Tarn below and Cofa Pike nearby. This is a great summit.

An old wall passes close to the east of the main cairn and provides a guide down to the head of Raise Beck in bad weather, and a faint path (that soon improves) heads off west to access the southern ridge. This ridge is spectacular and must rank as one of the Lakeland classic descent routes. I first used it on a winter's night many years ago after deciding to climb Seat Sandal following a day on the Helvellyn range. It was a rash choice to make as I had only half an hour of daylight left when I arrived at Grisedale Tarn and the temperature was already well below freezing. However, it was a toss up between a cramponned descent down the frozen Raise Beck in fading light, or foolishly snatching yet another top before the day ended.

I have got myself in trouble on many occasions by doing this on a winter's nights, but this was not one of them. I had wanted to descend the southern ridge of Seat Sandal for a while and once on the summit, I decided to go for it. The light went shortly after I began to head down and there was little sign of a path in those days, but I had a head torch and compass and the lights of Grasmere in the valley below provided a good guide for the general direction. As well as that there was a fast rising full moon and it was a clear night so there was no drama. The only down side was the fact I was parked at Dunmail Raise and once I had followed the intake walls and fences to pick up Tongue Gill, I had a noisy half hour walking back up the main road to my parked car.

I have since found a way of avoiding this road walk and it has become my favourite route on this fell. It is however a short route, suitable for afternoons or morning outings only, and if you want a longer day try coming here from Patterdale via Birks and St Sunday's Crag. Descend to Grisedale Tarn and you will have Seat Sandal ahead of you. If you follow the left (south side) of Grisedale Tarn, you can pick up a rough path beside the broken wall that follows Gavel Crag to the summit. Descend north by the wall to the head of Raise Beck and go round the other side of the tarn to take the excellent path past Ruthwaite Lodge and down Grisedale back to Patterdale. It's about ten miles and a glorious outing.

However you choose to climb to this forgotten summit, let's give 'Billy-no-mates' a boost. This is a fell that deserves much better from all of us.

But for a real flavour of this fell in about five rough miles try this: park in Dunmail Raise lay-by and cross the stile but ignore the path towards Raise Beck and head uphill to the wall above the buildings on the right. Follow this intake wall on its left where a faint path/sheeptrack will help. When the wall drops right head half left to cross rough ground and bracken (trackless) and pick up the good path on the southern ridge. Follow this to the summit and then follow the broken wall north to Raise Beck. Go left and make the rough descent back to the road and return to your car.

NOTE – the bracken is often high in summer between leaving the wall and reaching the south ridge. If this is the case it may be better to follow the wall and curve around to join the ridge lower down. It involves a bit of lost height but is a feasible alternative.

MADE TO BE CLIMBED

The lofty mass of Black Combe is one of the most easily identifiable summits in Lakeland and is known to the general public as much as to regular walkers. Strange then, that the fell should be less popular than many others in the Lakes, even though it falls within the boundaries of the National Park.

I believe there are two contributing factors to this – the first, and least important, is that poor Black Combe falls 30 feet below the magical 2,000 feet mark that would have put it on a lot of peak baggers' tick lists. And secondly, and very significantly, is the fact that Alfred Wainwright omitted it from his *Pictorial Guides*, and by doing so condemned it to a life of fell walking obscurity. He put the matter partly right by giving the fell sixteen pages in his 'mopping up' work *The Outlying Fells of Lakeland* (the unofficial eighth book in the series), but unfortunately for Black Combe, the damage was already well and truly done.

And yet Wainwright was surprisingly fond of this top, writing, "Black Combe was made to be climbed, and climbed it should be. It is considerate to the old and infirm; the grass bridleway to its summit from Whicham is amongst the most delectable of Lakeland fell paths. Which other can be ascended in carpet slippers?"

He was referring here to most popular ascent of the fell from near Whicham Church just off the A595 where a delectable, wide grassy path makes a smooth ascent and descent a joy. This is surely the way most people climb the fell, going up and down the same way and enjoying a jolly good outing in the bargain?

I would also like to suggest for the magnificent ascent up Whitecombe Beck from Beckside Farm a little over two miles east of Whicham, where a frequently ignored track winds beside Whitecombe Beck into magnificently wild and remote terrain under the imposing crags of Blackcombe and Whitecombe's scree. This is an ascent that will delight you and have you wondering how you ever missed it out of your Lakeland days before. A neat circuit can be made by following the beck to its head near Stoupdale Head and then heading west to the summit of Black Combe on a good track with great views south, returning by picking a (mostly) trackless descent down the eastern shoulder of the fell keeping well away from the drop of Blackcombe's scree as you do so. This is not a recommended way in mist (as we found out on our last visit) as the odd bits of track there come and go and in trying to avoid the crags it's all too easy to venture too far south and end up having to descend very steep rough ground in the vicinity of Sty Knotts.

But choose a day of sunshine and you will find yourself completing a wonderful circuit of around five and half miles and again you will begin to wonder why you've never been here before. It's a pity you can't combine the two routes mentioned above without some unpleasant road walking at the beginning or the end – but you can't. The best solution if you want to try it is to use two cars and take the stress and pain out of it by parking one at each start point, walking up Whitecombe Beck (my preferred way) and back down to Whicham and a waiting car to ferry you back to the other vehicle.

There are other routes of ascent – a track can be picked up from the A595 near Holegill Bridge and followed to Holegill Beck where it heads north before taking a long sweep south to climb the north western shoulder of Black Combe. And there is also a long trudge from the summit of the Fell Road close to Stoneside Hill, but this can be dreary in anything less than perfect weather.

What you'll get if you take time to come here is lots of space and magnificent views. You very rarely get crowds on Black Combe and the view from the summit is extensive.

It was believed for a long time to be the highest mountain in England and when looked at from the nearby coast it is easy to understand why. Black Combe is a great bulk of a mountain that quite simply looks huge – and Wainwright was quite right, it simply begs to be climbed and it should be – at least once in a fell walking lifetime. However, I suspect if you give it a go you will make many return visits – I first climbed it about fifteen years ago and have been back often.

Black Combe had many fans apart from Wainwright. William Wordsworth praised the view from the top and was the first (I believe) to make the claim that from the summit you got the longest continuous view in England over land – that being all the way to near Jack Hill close to Hanley in Staffordshire. In writing this he said, "the amplest range of unobstructed prospect may be seen that British ground commands". The Lakeland Poet, the late Norman Nicholson, was also very fond of the view of the fell from his Millom home and that sage of Lakeland writers Harry Griffin was proud to tell that Black Combe had been his first proper mountain climb (he grew up in Barrow). Indeed, it remained a favourite of his throughout his life and he never changed his view that the fell should be classed as a 'mountain' despite its lack of a few feet. The summit of Black Combe is a magical place. A large wind shelter and trig point sit on a vast flat grassy plateau (claimed by Wainwright to be perfect for a football pitch!) and a short walk to the east brings you to the abrupt downfall of Blackcombe's scree while a second well built southern cairn on the subsidiary summit marks one of the best viewpoints for the sea and coast that seem to fill the view as one stands here. The summit has often been used as a beacon site, a testament to its prominence in the surrounding landscape.

And the view of Lakeland itself is no less impressive with all the major fells including Scafell Pike, Skiddaw and Helvellyn being in your sights. It's a breathtaking panorama and would make the climb worthwhile if there was nothing else to recommend this top to walkers, but there is. The climb up is enough to get you puffing and make you realise you are climbing a 'proper top' and not just something Wainwright added as an afterthought to fill an eighth book!

Black Combe is a true mountain in every sense of the word. It is claimed that you can see fourteen counties from the summit – but I am not sure how you could identify them all and substantiate this! Harry Griffin insisted it was possible, on a clear day, to see the Isle of Man, the mountains of Snowdonia and some of the Irish peaks from the summit cairn. Black Combe is also claimed to be visible from Blackpool's North Pier, from numerous points along the Fylde Coast and even from the top of the two great cathedrals in Liverpool way to the south. I once spoke to a man who swore he had several times been able to see the Irish ferry leaving Holyhead (on Anglesey) for Dublin from the top and my father, a life long seaman, tells me it is often visible from ships leaving the port at Liverpool and heading into the Irish Sea.

All of this is possibly true on the right sort of day, but one irrefutable fact is that Black Combe consists largely of Skiddaw slate which geologists will tell you is one of the oldest rocks in the world; so we can add to Black Combe's list of claims that it was not only considered the highest mountain in England at one time but it can actually be truthfully said that it is one of the oldest in not only England, but probably the world.

Well, if all this doesn't make you head for Beckside or Whicham this Saturday, I am at a loss to just what will. Go and give Black Combe a go and see just what you are missing – but chose your day with care. The fell's close proximity to the sea means it often has its own weather micro-climate working and can be cloud topped when all around is clear. Don't let that put you off though.

Let's finish with some lines from Norman Nicholson who saw Black Combe more than most (and in all weathers) from his study window in Millom. "Black Combe alone still hides", he wrote in his poetry anthology *Sea to the West*, "and beneath the Herdwick Fleece of mist you can feel the heave of the hill".

And with those simple sentiments he gives us as graphic a description as we could wish for of the sheer presence and bulk of this great Lakeland summit.

THE WELCOME HOME FELL

There is one summit I always look forward to spotting on my journeys south down the M6, be it from a business trip to Glasgow or Edinburgh or after one of my many Munro bagging excursions to the Highlands. They've turned into a long term project for me due to the distance I have to travel, and my original estimate of ten years has now changed and I anticipate a finish date of somewhere around my sixtieth birthday!

I often find myself heading down the M6 from Gretna direction and after the long slog through the southern uplands I know I am getting close to Lakeland when I pick out the distinctive sloping ridge of Carrock Fell ahead and to the west. I always look for it and unless the rain is hammering down and the clag low, I pick it out a little north of Carlisle and on days of good visibility I can usually spot it before I cross the border from Scotland.

Of all the mountains on the eastern fringes of the Lakes, Carrock Fell is one of the most distinctive from either the motorway or the fells around the Pooley Bridge end of Ullswater. And to be fair, it really is a cracking summit with a little bit of everything for the fell walker. At 2,174 feet it's a reasonable height and has easy ways up as well as demanding and steep routes. I have always thought of it as one of the more aggressive fells of the Lake District – prickly and irritable with a mean streak that shows in bad weather. However, I have spent many great times on and around its slopes on sunny days and found it a place to linger and relax.

My first ascent was a solo effort on a foul winter's day of blustery snow and freezing weather. The Lakes had looked bleak and unpleasant from the moment I arrived and my planned ascent of Blencathra's Sharp Edge was postponed as my partner for the day had failed to turn up and I didn't fancy it much on my own in the dreadful conditions. Looking to snatch something from the time I had remaining, I headed down past Mungrisdale and parked on the rough moor near Stone Ends Farm a little past Mosedale.

I hadn't climbed many of the northern fells at that point and saw them as dull grassy mounds, but someone had told me that Carrock Fell was the exception to this rule. Determined to find out for myself, I set off alone – there was no one else out and about on that particular day – and went up and down the same way following the faint path (or at least it was then!) that cuts diagonally across the gabbro rocks of the nasty looking east face of the fell. What a revelation it turned out to be!

There were some tricky rock steps to negotiate (made much

worse by being ice covered) and lots of steep ground with a bit of exposure thrown in too. And the upper slopes, although of a gentler angle, were snow covered and presented a challenge with hidden rocks below. The path vanished around here and I almost lost my nerve in the white-out conditions between the east peak and the summit. I touched the fine rock pillar on the top and then raced back down and on to a café in Penrith to warm up, pleased with my short adventure. I know you will say that I didn't do the fell justice with this 'smash and grab' approach and I would agree with you although in my defence, I have returned here often using this top as a start or end to much longer days on the other hills hereabouts.

When reviewing his *Northern Fells* book, Wainwright is complimentary about Carrock Fell claiming that it was an "exception" to the general form of the fells in this area of Lakeland and that "it would rank high in any company". And so it would. This is a real Maverick summit and the highest bits are a true mountain top with two ends and good stony plateau in between. The western summit is the higher and has a wonderful stone pillar set on a rocky plinth overlooking a wild scene of surrounding fells and valleys with High Pike and Blencathra both prominent.

If you are lucky enough to get cloud whisping over the slanting ridge between you and the eastern top it looks very atmospheric and you would be forgiven for thinking you had found yourself on some high and remote summit in the wilder parts of Norway. There is a sense of being far from everything here even though the road can be seen below. The feeling of height comes from the fact that Carrock Fell is one of the terminations of high ground in this area of Lakeland. East of here the ground stays low over the vale of Eden and looks very dramatic.

Back to the summit however, and apart from the view (which is very impressive) the other attraction here is the ancient Iron Age hill fort that can be seen ringing the edges of the plateau. It is fairly complete and has four gaps in it which appear to correspond to the main points of the compass and are believed by many historians to be the entry points to the fort. I have read (in other descriptions by those who know about these things) that they are also believed to be the areas where the wall defences were breached during battles. It is hard to imagine this peaceful spot besieged and people dying here, but if the latter theory is correct, then it must have happened. All is tranquil now but the remains of the fort are a reminder of past times and to be fair, it is great fun to sit up here and visualise just who lived in such an elevated place and the conditions they must have endured. One theory suggests that the fort was a central gathering point for rebels in the north in their struggle against the Roman occupying forces. Whatever the true facts, they are lost in the mists of time and we can only guess at what might have been.

And speaking of bad weather, for a fell that is basic and uncomplicated without numerous ridges, this can be a confusing place when the clag comes down. My first experience in the heavy snow was not the only time I have been forced to reach for the compass to guide me in this vicinity. It seems I am in good company too as that ardent and original fell walker and Lakeland poet Samuel Taylor Coleridge also got lost in mist here as did the author Charles Dickens who, along with his friend Wilkie Collins, had a difficult time finding their way down.

You do need to be careful. To the north and the west it is not too bad as steep ground can be descended safely enough back to the base, but the east has rough crags and the south has steep broken ground that needs to be traversed with great care, if at all. I like to do a small horseshoe when I walk here and I have outlined it below as I believe the fell has more to offer than just ascending it up and down from the east the same way.

There is much here too for those who are not summit baggers or fell walkers. There is a plethora of geological fun to be had in the vicinity for those who like such things.

To the west the River Caldew is one of the few places where the pink looking Skiddaw Granite is exposed and I am told that the fell is where the sedimentary rock that includes Skiddaw's shale and slate is crushed against the volcanic gabbros that form the base of this top. If you have climbed in Skye on the Cuillin you will be familiar with the wonderful rough qualities of gabbro, but it is very rare in Lakeland.

And then there are the mines. This was a rich area for mining and Carrock Fell is famous in the history of Lakeland mining and known for having many rich mineral veins and some metal ones too. The rare wolfram was extracted from the Carrock Mine which is (or was) situated in a side valley of the Caldew where Brandy Gill and Grainsgill Beck meet. If you like exploring rough ground you will love it around here. I have to say as well that I have seen more foxes around Carrock Fell than in any other area of the Lakes. I have no idea of why this should be, but it has to be said that if they were looking for good bolt holes to escape from man, then the fell is full of great places for them to hide.

Carrock Fell is a superb outing. Wainwright ranks it second only to Blencathra in the *Northern Fells* which is high praise indeed. It's one of those fells where an ascent can be made rough or easy depending on your mood at the time and that's something that can't be said of too many other tops in Lakeland as a whole.

The best way to appreciate this fell is to visit another top first – that being High Pike. I usually park in the vicinity of Carrock Beck near the ford on the road. From here good mine tracks lead up to the 2,157 feet summit of High Pike. Be careful after Sandbed Mine to take the correct path to get to the summit and not the good track that traverses under it. From High Pike, two wonderful miles take you below Drygill Head, past Red Gates (where a good path takes you back down if the weather turns), over Milton Hill and on to the summit of Carrock Fell.

To return to the start you can either back track down the way you came to pick up a good traversing path that cuts right (north east) under the summit or (and this is my preferred option) just head north down the fell side. It's rough and steep and a bit wet in the lower parts, but on a clear day provides a wonderful end to a great round.

Big Brother is Watching You

It was the nearest I have ever come to seeing a full blown cloud inversion in Lakeland. I have looked longingly at the breathtaking photos that you see in climbing and walking books depicting little 'islands' of mountain tops sticking out of seas of white fluffy clouds that lap like be-calmed water around them, and have watched weather patterns eagerly to try and witness this spectacular performance for myself. But in twenty years of trying, the closest I ever came was on this particular late October morning on the summit of Catstycam.

A friend and I had left Glenridding very early and in the dark to try to catch the phenomena that all the signs looked good for, and had arrived on the summit of this much neglected and lovely fell shortly after the sun rose, anticipating mouth watering photo opportunities. Sadly they never materialised. We knew we were near the upper limits of the low cloud and clag that swirled around us, the milky, early sunlit sky was tantalisingly close and from time to time a dark shape loomed out of the mist in the direction of Helvellyn, but it never cleared enough to give us what we came for.

However, we were high up early on what was going to be a glorious mid-autumn day and that was compensation enough. What made the morning so memorable though, was the party of lively Scousers that appeared, ghost-like out of the mist below us and crowded onto the summit of Catstycam. We had heard them coming for some time below with raised voices and much swearing, but we weren't quite expecting the nine sweaty bodies that suddenly appeared to shatter our early morning contemplation. "Mornin' boss", the burley leader threw at us as they shuffled for position. As summits go, Catstycam is a classic one; a real pointy place with little room for more than a couple of people and yet somehow this party managed to 're-group' all around us and spew out flasks and even a little stove from bulging rucksacks.

We got to talking although we really wanted to move on and get back to the peace and quiet. I am from Liverpool myself, so recognizing a fellow Liverpudlian the party warmed to us. It was only when the leader asked us to take a photo of them all that we realised we had a dilemma. "We'll all group around the top like," he told me, "first time up Helvellyn for all us y'see." Now that is always a tricky one. A party in high spirits on the wrong mountain but thinking they were somewhere else has to be handled carefully. If you do it wrong the leader, feeling stupid, comes down on you like the wrath of God. They took it well – if you count violent swearing and name calling of said leader to be good natured!

But you see that's the thing about Catstycam. It's such a big and impressive mountain that a lot of people climb it and think it is Helvellyn. And let's face it, and I'll probably ruffle a few feathers when I say this, as the two summits go, this is a far better one than Helvellyn which promises much on the ascent but has only a flat plateau to offer once you are there. True enough, it has the height and the superb vistas to Swirral Edge and Striding Edge and awesome drops to Red Tarn, but if you like your tops small and pointy – just like a child would draw one on a piece of paper – then Catstycam is the top for you. The problem this fell has is that it will always live in the shadow of its bigger brother and never achieve the status it truly deserves. Let's face it, how many summits can you name of over 2,900 feet that get regularly by-passed and ignored in Lakeland by those who walk and climb there on a regular basis?

Not many; but this has always been Catstycam's fate and probably always will be. The party I mentioned earlier are not on their own in the mistake they made although I have to say, they did well to lose the good path to Red Tarn and pick up the very indistinct (this was over ten years ago) path that leaves it to climb the east shoulder of this fell. Nowadays this path is much more distinct, but it would still take iron determination to leave the wide and obvious track around the base of Catstycam to take the much smaller path up to this lower summit.

I recall a more recent winter's day with hard ground and snow on the tops of the highest fells when I left the summit of Catstycam in thick mist and full winter gear to bump almost immediately into a middle aged woman who was quite perplexed that the ground had risen up steeply after her descent of Swirral Edge instead of carrying on downwards.

I explained that she had climbed up to the top of Catstycam in error and she looked at me in horror. "I never stopped to check my map," she said, "but I never realised there was another big summit so close to Helvellyn"! She walked back down with me to the junction with the Red Tarn path. She was charming company and when we parted she still seemed bemused. Her dilemma is similar to many other people's. They are blinkered to the delights and possibilities of Helvellyn and all around is seen as being 'just a part' of that mountain.

Poor old Catstycam. By a freak of geography this wonderful fell has been robbed of its cult status and relegated into almost total oblivion. I couldn't agree more with Wainwright when he writes about Catstycam as follows – "If Catstycam stood alone, remote from its fellows, it would be one of the finest peaks in Lakeland". He continues, "it has nearly, but not quite, the perfect mountain form, with true simplicity in its soaring lines, and a small pointed top, a real summit". Wainwright was not known for his conservative views but I think even he may have understated it a bit here.

Stop and think for a minute and see if you can come up with a more mountain looking mountain in Lakeland (or anywhere in England for that matter) than Catstycam. You'll be hard pushed. This pointy top is an easily identifiable peak from a lot of points of the Lakes and like Great Gable, always looks impressive.

During my Munro bagging days in Scotland we play the game of 'spotting Schiehallion' which has a similar pointy top when seen from many views and is visible from many areas of the Highlands. We play a similar game with Catstycam in the Lakes. We get a childish pride from being the first to point it out on Lakeland days.

Catstycam is a real mountain in every sense of the word, and cloaked in winter snow it takes on an almost Alpine appearance, especially if viewed from high on Birkhouse Moor where you would be mistaken for thinking it unclimbable in ice without ropes and associated gear.

I suppose it's all a sham really. In reality this wonderful top is connected to its big brother Helvellyn by a high ridge. But what a ridge to be 'one end' of! When you drop from the summit of Catstycam and Swirral Edge looms across the void it can be quite intimidating. Another appealing aspect the fell has is that the slopes are very dry no matter what the weather and the mixture of bright stones and short grass make it a most attractive climb from most points.

So how should you approach this summit if I have persuaded you to turn aside from its bigger brother and give it a second look? Most people ascend it to bag an extra 'Wainwright' as part of the ascent or descent of Helvellyn via Swirral Edge and follow the well worn path that climbs to the col above Red Tarn and below the scramble of the edge. From here a fair path meanders to the top.

I think a summit such as this deserves far more. If you must do it this way, at least search out the path up the east shoulder (or down it) that leaves the main Helvellyn path as it climbs by Red Tarn Beck. The path up here used to be indistinct but is now quite good. You will not find it hard and will be on grass all the way. The views all around are superb and as you get near the top and the angle eases, you get a feeling of real mountaineering as you gaze at the mountain scenery all around.

However, if you really want to do this fell justice there is only one 'proper' way. The north face of the mountain is rocky and impressive and the north western ridge is an obvious arrow like route to the summit. It is very steep and rough and near the top it is exposed and glorious. If you climb to the summit this way you will feel as though you have really climbed a decent sized mountain. Make a point of getting a few photos of this ridge from nearby Whiteside to show your friends as the gloat factor is high. It really looks almost impossible from here and to boast of an ascent will raise eyebrows! In reality, an intermittent path climbs all the way up the north western ridge and once found near the old dam of Kepplecove Tarn, the route is easy to follow.

Kepplecove Tarn is not really a tarn anymore but in wet weather is very muddy. It originally serviced the Glenridding lead mines but flooded and burst out of its hollow in October 1927 following a cloudburst. In 1931 the dam was holed and has remained the same ever since.

Guidebook writer Mark Richards states that the name Catstycam translates as "a hen-comb shaped crest with a steep path frequented by wild cat". That's quite a mouthful if someone asked you what your destination was for the day. I think Catstycam will do just fine. Big brother may be looking down, but like all older or larger siblings, I'll bet Helvellyn has many sleepless nights about its smaller neighbour growing in stature. Another hundred feet would do, and would probably leave big brother devoid of climbers.

Whichever way you choose to climb Catstycam, take the time to do it. When the sun shines and Helvellyn is a long line of summit bound walkers, take refuge here and watch the chaos from afar. You will find peace when 'big brother' is heaving with sweaty bodies.

THE OXYMORON MOUNTAIN

Late one mid-December afternoon some years ago my wife and I parked our car at the Hawse End car park and set out to climb Catbells. It was a day of howling winds and driving snow falling from bleak leaden grey skies, a true winter's day in every sense of the word. We had the car park to ourselves, not bad for a Saturday, but then when you considered the weather conditions it was hardly surprising. Our original intention had been to do a high level circuit of Coledale from Grisedale Pike to Causey Pike, but such a route was out of the question in the conditions. The Met office was issuing severe weather warnings and the snow ploughs were heading out of their garages while we sat gloomily in a café in Keswick already having spent far too much in the outdoor shops. And so, deciding to salvage something from the day, we headed for Catbells and what we hoped would be a quick and easy dash to the summit. Up the wonderful northern ridge, over the top, and down to Hause Gate with a return on the high level track along the flank of the fellside. Kids' stuff, really. Everyone knows how easy Catbells is, even Wainwright claimed that 'grannies' could climb it and at 1,481 feet, it was hardly high!

There was an hour and half of daylight left as we crossed the road at the top of the car park and began the steep climb up the ridge. The wind strength grew steadily as we climbed and the snow flakes were huge and swirled in blizzardy whirls around us. The path had long been obliterated but we knew the way well enough even in those near white out conditions. Once we passed the memorial tablet at about 1,000 feet, things really started to get nasty. Visibility dropped to almost nothing and when the ferocious wind did tear the brooding clag around us apart, we looked down on a Borrowdale in the full grip of winter. On both sides of the ridge lights were already on in the houses below as we battled our way slowly along the flatter part before the final steep rise to the summit. Communication was all but impossible as we had our hoods pulled tightly around our faces to keep out the stinging snow and the merciless wind. Crampons were useless as the snow was too soft and we used ice axes more for support than for anything else.

Huddling together for shelter and stability by the final rock step below the summit we had long ago abandoned the thought of traversing the top, our revised aim being merely to summit and then get the hell out of there. Now if anyone had told me before this I would one day fail to get to the top of Catbells, I would have laughed. But pride really does come before a fall.

As we stood the wind hit gale force and flattened us against the rock, the snow became a wall of white and we had no choice but to retreat. Our descent down the ridge was hairy to say the least and in parts we resorted to crawling to keep moving. It was two very sorry individuals who arrived back home that evening. Sorry, but certainly a lot wiser.

So far in this chapter we have tended to look at the less popular and sometimes, less glamorous of the Lakeland tops and point out their redeeming features, but Catbells is very famous and incredibly popular and well climbed by all age groups. But a note of caution is needed here, for Catbells is a funny mountain. And mountain I will call it. Forget all this 2,000 feet status for the point at which a 'hill' becomes a 'mountain'. I go along with Wainwright on this; it's not about height, it's about ruggedness and the summit itself.

Catbells is rugged alright and has a true and airy mountain summit. But when I hear people refer to 'easy Catbells' I smile to myself and have come to label it 'the oxymoron mountain'. Simple it can be, but it depends on the day, on the conditions, on the route.

I remember another time on a gorgeous spring Sunday evening when a group of us stood on the rocky summit looking over the northern lakes at a scene of sublime loveliness. There were no clouds in the sky and not a ripple on Derwentwater. The sun was warm and there was no wind. It had been a great weekend. We had backpacked up from Coniston over numerous tops and this was our last one. Someone passed the Mars Bars around and far below we watched the ferry pull away from Hawse End jetty. It was six o' clock and instead of marching back to Keswick we decided to make a quick dash back to the base of the ridge and catch the next ferry to the town. It would be the perfect end to a great trip.

We reckoned the next ferry would be about six thirty, in our ignorance, and worse, we figured we could easily get down the northern ridge in that half hour, backpacks or not. Catbells was just about to teach us another lesson! That descent is not as easy as you think.

We arrived grumpy and sore at almost seven having had our pride well and truly dented. Progress down the rougher parts of the ridge, those little rock steps, can be slow indeed. As it turned out we sat at the landing stage for another hour before we accosted a dog walking local who informed us that the last ferry had been the one we had watched depart from the summit at six. It would be another few weeks before they switched to their summer schedule.

It was a disgruntled party who arrived in Keswick after dark that evening, communication having ceased in all but grunts and odd nods of the head. A fell for grannies indeed!

Perhaps the most remarkable thing that ever happened to me on Catbells occurred early one September day. Gary and I often met up for early morning routes. Both of us had busy daily schedules but found we walked well together and would set off before dawn to complete a circuit and still give ourselves the rest of the day for dreaded work. This morning we had planned to circuit Newlands from Maiden Moor to Hindscarth and had struggled up in the dark from Little Town. On reaching Hause Gate we couldn't resist including Catbells so we set off up it in the half light of what was going to be a glorious autumn day. We were only half way there when we both stopped dead in our tracks. Ahead, on the top, was a figure, a woman. We couldn't make out details from the distance we were at but she seemed to be dressed in a long flowing gown of bright white. We looked at each other and looked back but she was gone. We were younger then and we sprinted to the top. There was nothing. No sign that anyone had been there and no sign of anyone heading down the ridge.

It certainly sent a shiver down my spine and I have often pondered since what exactly we did see. If it was a trick of the light we both saw exactly the same thing at precisely the same time. I have no explanation for it and when I tell people the story they look at me as if I am making it up. But it happened and it happened on Catbells.

As for Gary, the last time we were together was on Catbells. We had walked from Buttermere together over Fleetwith Pike, Dale Head, High Spy and Maiden Moor. For some reason I can't remember I was parked at Hawse End and he at Little Town. We drank coffee with the summit to ourselves in the gathering gloom of an October evening and watched the lights come on around Derwentwater. Then shaking hands we parted to head back to our cars.

As I looked back at him silhouetted against the Lake I somehow knew I would never see him again. I never did. We had decided to meet a month later in Kentmere, an arrangement that suited both of our work commitments. Gary never made it. Work sent him to South Africa and he fell in love with Cape Town. He had only a failed marriage to hold him in England and so he made the decision to change his life. He came back only once to put his affairs in order and we missed each other. We exchange cards at Christmas and I have often promised to go and visit but never have.

I think of him when I am on Catbells and pause often to reflect on that rocky summit and to remember the last time we were up there together. It seems now to belong to another life and not my own, but Catbells is the same as ever it was and I guess it always will be.

THE MOTORISTS' MOUNTAIN

About ten years ago I was fortunate enough to have a caravan just off the A66 between Penrith and Keswick at the quiet and remote caravan site at Troutbeck Head. We stayed there every weekend during the long summer season for the best part of two years until the owner, a wonderful Geordie called Bob, sold it to the Caravan Club and they redeveloped it for their own members.

I have many wonderful memories of our days there, but the two that are the most endearing are the magnificent view we had over the fields to Blencathra which filled our front window morning to night, and the fell that towered over the site looking impossibly steep from below. This was Great Mell Fell and over that period I came to know it, and its near neighbour, Little Mell Fell, as 'The Motorists' Mountains'.

I'll tell you why later; but let me share the story of the first day I climbed to what, in those days, was the remote and little visited summit of Great Mell Fell. We are talking about the mid 1990s here and this fell in particular was pretty inaccessible to walkers in the Lake District. True, it was National Trust property, but getting on the hill itself was the main problem as there was no real legal access to it. The few who did climb to the top used the cart track near Brownrigg Farm on the minor road running north east from Matterdale End. This entered National Trust land (of which the fell consisted) a short way up it over a rickety old stile. You never felt comfortable on that track as there was no official right of way and even when on the fell itself, there was always the feeling that maybe you shouldn't be there at all. This state of affairs persisted until quite recently.

Anyway, in those days and today as well, the main way to the top was up the whale back south eastern ridge that climbed attractively to the lovely summit. There was little path, just a sketchy track in a few places. Even with the caravan as a base, it was some time before I decided to explore the fell. We had spent our first few months in the area climbing any of the northern fells we had not been up before and although I had been tempted by the steep sides of Great Mell Fell, I had left it alone, discouraged by the access problem.

One glorious summer's morning in early June I finally put the matter to right. Creeping from the caravan around five o' clock I walked off the site and followed the road for the long slog to the cart track. Great Mell Fell is circled around its base by a great track that can be left anywhere once you are on it and the summit reached by a sweaty and panting pull up the unbelievably steep slopes. Obviously the easier graded ridge was simpler, but once I gained the fell side on that morning I stayed on the low track until I reached the northern end of the fell and then simply climbed the trackless ground to the summit. Sounds easy? Don't be fooled! The 600 feet or so of ascent you encounter at this point is as near vertical in places as you would wish to get without resorting to using your hands. Looking between your legs as you climbed gave you vertigo. But it was worth it. I reached the summit at about half six and the northern lakes glowed in the early morning June sunshine. There was no one else on the fell and I sat for an hour in the warmth by the small pile of stones that marked the top and marvelled at the view of the Dodds and Clough Head, but most of all I couldn't take my eyes off the magnificent panorama of Blencathra.

People rant about the view of this mountain from Clough Head but I have to tell you, the picture that greets you when you reach Great Mell Fell's summit takes some beating. I found it hard to tear myself away on that first visit. The High Street Fells looked close enough to touch, Grisedale Pike and Hopegill Head towered over the Vale of Keswick and the Cross Fell Plateau looked as though someone had painted it on a blue canvas. I came down the back, the easy way, but forsook the road and went around the base on the cart track to indulge in a small trespass over the rough marshy ground that Rookin House Activity Centre used at the time for driving tanks and diggers around for those longing to try such things.

That first visit set the standard for many others but it would be almost a year before I set eyes on anyone else on that wonderful summit. It was late April and I had decided to grab a quick ascent on a gorgeous spring evening instead of wasting it in front of the caravan T.V. I climbed directly up the west side and as always on those steeper edges, the summit appears almost like a jack in the box. One minute you are battling with impossibly steep slopes, the next you over the crest, on the summit, with the view hitting you in the face.

On that particular evening I dragged myself upright, out of breath as usual and came face to face with a party of three drinking coffee at the cairn. We all looked at each other in stunned silence. "You're the only person we've ever seen up here," one of the two ladies said. "Ditto" I replied. I am not sure if we were disappointed or just shell shocked but we shared coffee and biscuits and played name the fell for an hour before descending in the dark together and they very kindly gave me a lift back to Troutbeck Head.

Things have changed a little now. The new access laws have made it easier to justify being on Great Mell and its smaller brother Little Mell Fell, but you still feel a little uneasy...maybe it's a historical thing.

So why 'The Motorists' Mountains'? Neither summit tops the magic 2,000 feet mark so they don't really qualify as mountains anyway (although as we mentioned in an earlier chapter, that very much depends on your viewpoint!) Well, be that as it may, I don't think the two 'Mell Fells' realise it! If a requirement for a mountain is steepness and good summit views (and I know it isn't really!), then both these tops are in that league. The title came about because when people came to visit us at the caravan we always told them to watch for the two tops as they approached down the A66 and that the site was directly underneath Great Mell Fell. I have met a lot of people who associate arriving in the northern lakes with their first view of these two summits as they motor down the A66. Many have never climbed them, putting them in the category of 'must do some day'. But they mark the beginning of a day in an area they love and they mark the final minutes at day's end when you are heading back to the M6.

I have to recommend these two to all who have never climbed them however. They are worth far more than just being sentinels to mark an exit and entry point. And they still have the added bonus of being relatively quiet when a lot of Lakeland summits see more traffic than ever. Both are now to a larger degree 'access land' and although you may never be able to make a ten mile route out of either of them, they will still provide you with endless days of good mountain fun and many memories. The views from both are really great, but particularly so from Great Mell Fell. They also often miss the worst of the weather on bad days as they are alone and isolated and the higher linked ranges all around seem to hold it. The result? You can grab a day when foul conditions keep you off other tops. You may be down a bit earlier but that just gives a bit more time for the pub, right?

The best way up Great Mell Fell is still by the south eastern ridge with a complete traverse taking you over the top and down the northern slopes to return on that marvellous cart track. But do be careful. Those slopes really are very steep and in ice or wet they are treacherous and demand respect.

For Little Mell Fell the royal way is to climb on the good path from The Hause on the high angled road out of Watermillock near Ullswater. Again, this is very steep but the summit is soon reached. It is probably as well to go back the same way, there are various extensions you can make to this but all take you off access land at some point and the legality of your position begins to make you uneasy.

In Wainwright's day there was a military firing range below the northern slopes but this has long gone and you can spend your days here in relative peace. But don't take my word for it, go and give it a try for yourself. The only intrusion you will get into your wanderings will be the odd solitary walker you may encounter. Please don't be rude to them though, the chances are one of them will be me.

When Small is Beautiful

I would like to finish this chapter on mountain profiles by looking at something a bit different. So far we have considered individual mountains and expounded on their many and varied merits. But the Lake District has numerous what can best be termed 'mini mountains' – some less than 1,000 feet in height and some more. All share one thing in common and that is that they are often overlooked by the masses for reasons that may become clear as we take time to look at them.

There is a certain col with a small parking area at the head of Dunnerdale a few impressive miles above Broughton Mills, where I like to park from time to time, I'm sure you probably know where I mean. It is remote and never really gets as packed as many of the Lakeland parking areas, but that's not the reason I go there. It's an atmospheric place be it on a spring day of blue skies and fresh winds or a brooding winter's afternoon of lowering skies and odd snow flurries. It is also the starting point for a very quick ascent of that wonderful 'mini mountain' Stickle Pike. A short half mile will see you panting up a decent track past lovely Stickle Tarn, nestling in its sheltered hollow, and then diverting off to climb steeply and roughly up the front of this oft neglected Lakeland top. It can be done from the car in half an hour, there and back, if the mood takes you. But even on a day of bad weather there are few who would don boots and not take longer, lingering and dreaming on Stickle Pike's rocky summit. The fell may be small in stature but at the top you will find the rugged summit of a true mountain and one that many a higher height would be proud of and gladly exchange its own featureless plateau for.

'Mini mountains' as I have christened the likes of Stickle Pike, are more common than you may think in Lakeland and for years I was blinded to their existence by my pursuit of the glories of Blencathra, Great Gable and their like. What, I would argue, could anything that took less than an hour out of the car, have to offer hardened fell walkers who only think a day worthwhile if the mileage gets over ten? With age comes experience and more importantly wisdom, and looking back I can now see how mistaken I was.

The likes of Stickle Pike are true classic summits and what they lack in height and mileage they make up for in ruggedness and character and truly wonderful tops.

And that's the secret here. When I call them 'mini mountains' I am perhaps being a bit unkind to them. Stickle Pike is 1,231 feet high so is not really a tiddler, even by Lakeland's standards. What I am trying to get at is that although these tops fall well short of the normal idea of mountain status in stature, height and ascent, they never the less have summits and routes up them that qualify them for that grand title.

Standing on the small rocky summit of Stickle Pike, who could doubt for one moment that you were not atop a mountain? And if you didn't know better you would think it was one of some importance and great altitude. The rocky ground drops away all around you, there is not much room to move around and you have worked hard to get here in the first place.

I have come to love these summits. At first I used them as 'face savers' – places to come and grab a quick top to salvage a day when everything had gone wrong. We all have times like that. The weather goes against you and doesn't clear up until late afternoon, there are accidents on the motorway on the way or your mate over sleeps and you arrive three hours later than you should have. But I quickly learnt I was doing these peaks an injustice. They had so much more to offer me than just a vain charge up and down to make sure I could go home having 'bagged' a top and not 'wasted' a Lakeland day. Here I could enjoy a true mountain experience without the need to push hard to get there whilst keeping an eye on the weather and the time with a view to getting back in one piece and with enough hours remaining to fit whatever else needed cramming into an overfilled life.

On a summit such as Stickle Pike I can relax. There are seldom crowds on these tops as they are not as popular as their bigger brothers and you usually don't need to panic as to whether or not you will get a place in the car park if you are a little late. I can take out my flask feeling I have reached a true mountain summit and take in the skyline all around. And then I can decide if I want to go on and extend my day or if I am happy to meander back to the car waiting below and head off to the nearest café and treat myself to a bacon buttie!

Wainwright had a soft spot for true mountain tops be they small or large. He wrote that "mountain summits are especially attractive when they are rocky, abrupt on all sides, small in extent and exciting". That about sums it up – he was writing about the aforementioned Stickle Pike just as a matter of interest!

Wainwright really liked Stickle Pike singing its praises in *Outlying Fells*. If it had been in say, the fourth book *The Southern Fells* it would now have a reconstructed path up to the summit and you would probably have to wait your turn to step on to the top most inches as crowds thronged around.

I have found a great deal of pleasure in seeking out 'mini mountains' and love to take others there and watch their reactions when they lose their scepticism on reaching a good rocky mountain summit with such little effort. They are not unique to Lakeland, in fact in the likes of Snowdonia and Scotland, most don't even have paths up as the attractions of the numerous 3,000 feet mountains in these regions really does mean they get ignored. So maybe you should give one of them a go the next time you find yourself in Lakeland. And I don't mean just squeeze one in because it's past lunch and you really ought to get back to Keswick because your Gore-Tex trousers now have a small rip in them!

Going back to Wainwright, on writing about lowly Castle Crag in Borrowdale that doesn't even top 1,000 feet (but is a perfect example of what we are getting at here) he says, "if a visitor to Lakeland has only two or three hours to spare, poor fellow, and yet desperately wants to reach a summit and take back an enduring memory of the beauty and atmosphere of the district...let him climb Castle Crag".

Well, that's what we were talking about before, and although it has a time and a place for us all, I hope you treat the venture and adventure of 'mini mountains' in the spirit I have tried to suggest. Go with the intention of climbing one. Don't have a time scale, don't just fit it in because the weather isn't up to Helvellyn along Striding Edge, but go and sit on the summit and see how things develop. You'll be glad you did and pleasantly surprised at the results. And you will have found a new way of exploring some of the areas you very rarely visit in the Lakes.

Here are a few suggestions of 'mini mountains' for you to try. They all have the attributes of decent mountain summits with short and rough approaches:

STICKLE PIKE from the head of Dunnerdale.

GUMMERS How from the car park on the Newby Bridge to Bowland Bridge Road.

HIGH RIGG from the Church of St Johns in the Vale.

CASTLE CRAG from Borrowdale – popular anyway but has to be included.

CAW from Seathwaite in the Duddon Valley.

V.

LAKELAND LITERATURE

No other outdoor area in the United Kingdom (and possibly in the world) has inspired such a diverse and wonderful range of literature, paintings and drawings as Lakeland. It must be something in the air that inspires those who visit or settle here to put pen to paper and wax lyrical about all they see and do. And down the centuries a lot of what has been written has achieved what can only be termed 'classic' status. Part of my own enjoyment of The Lake District has been to read and re-read the vast array of books available about the region. Many think only of Wordsworth and co., the Romantic Lakeland poets, when they consider the written work of the area, but it goes far beyond that. Guidebook writers such as Alfred Wainwright and other more general authors such as Harry Griffin, are well known household names in outdoor circles.

But there are numerous others who will provide you with hours of interesting and entertaining reading on the region you love. Many of these led fascinating lives and were hugely involved in Cumbrian life.

In this final chapter I would like to encourage you to extend your enjoyment of our fells and lakes by starting your own library of Lakeland books. I will use the term 'classic' often over the next few chapters because what I hope to do is take some of the many and varied authors the Lakes has produced and look at their works, perhaps singling out what I consider to be the best one, and also to outline their lives.

I hope you find this as interesting as I do and I hope it opens up new worlds for you in your continued love affair with Lakeland.

Some of these writers may be familiar to you, there will be ones you have heard of briefly or seen a book by, some may be completely unknown to you but they all share one thing in common – an undeniable skill for transferring to their readers the love and passion they have for this superb landscape.

LAKELAND'S MYSTERY AUTHOR

The literature of the Lakes is a kaleidoscope of wonderful volumes written by a plethora of colourful characters many of whom have become household names down the years. However, there are still several who remained unknown to the general public despite churning out large amounts of quality work. Let's start this chapter by looking at perhaps the most influential of these.

To get things going let me pose you a question. If I were to tell you that there was a Cumbrian author who wrote almost forty books on Lakeland and the outdoor regions of our country, who lived until he was seventy seven and was a true son of the region having been born near Kendal, would you be surprised you hadn't heard of him. Well, chances are you have some of his books on your bookshelves and although the author's name may have been noted by you, you've probably let it pass from your memory as there was absolutely nothing in print about him.

I am referring here to William Thomas Palmer or simply W.T. Palmer as you may know him. Palmer's books covered a wide variety of outdoor subjects on which he wrote with passion and sound knowledge – the countryside, the fells, walking, climbing, the people who worked in this environment, all came under his scrutiny and provided subject matter for his affluent pen. In his way, William Thomas Palmer could be considered a forerunner of the late Harry Griffin in terms of the content of what he produced, his accurate local detail and his knowledge of his subject. He died in 1954 and although there are numerous books we could choose to look at under the title of 'Lakeland Classics', I have chosen two volumes – *Odd Corners in English Lakeland* and its follow up *More Odd Corners in English Lakeland* to introduce us to Palmer. He was a prolific writer and his writing style was chatty and flowed freely over the pages bringing the area he loved to life for his readers. He never wrote to any set pattern and often books would come out in batches with longer gaps (three or four years) in between.

So why was he so unknown as an author? In his day his books sold well enough, many going into several editions, and his writing career spanned an enormous time, from 1903 until 1952. His colourful descriptions gave his readers a rare insight into the world of the Lakes during those more innocent times and his down to earth accounts of the region and those who peopled it make wonderful reading. His genius was not just restricted to Lakeland and he wrote with conviction and knowledge on many other regions including Scotland, the Peak District, Wales and even areas down south.

His biographer, Sheila Richardson, in her book *The Forgotten Man of Lakeland*, writes that Palmer was "a man ahead of his time" an author with a prolific output but living in world that was pre-mass circulation, with no TV and commercial radio to give his efforts the coverage they deserved and this was almost certainly a contributing factor to his obscurity. There was also the small fact that in 1955 (the year after Palmer died) another Kendal man, one Alfred Wainwright, shot to the public's attention with his first *Pictorial Guide*!

William Palmer was born at Bowston near Kendal on 8 July 1877 and died on 26 February 1954. He went to school in neighbouring Burneside from 29 July 1882 until he left on 30 September 1892. He was an average student who achieved average results, and like other locals he was expected to take up employment in the local paper mill. His family were from a farming background and used to hard work but, unlike his parents, William spent his childhood reading books and walking as much as he could. Life was hard and money only available for essentials so he found himself forced to borrow books from older local people who were lucky enough to have them. One book he read was an early Lakeland guidebook containing maps and this probably set the young Palmer on the path he was to follow for the rest of his life. Starting with his 'local valleys' of Mardale and Kentmere, he began to explore Lakeland and take note of all he saw. It was these early wanderings that gave him most of his material for the books he produced in later life, and if the adage of writing only what you have experience of is true, it certainly applied to Palmer who had hands on experience of most aspects of outdoor life. He stayed fit and active all his life and loved to walk huge distances, he was also tee-total.

Starting his working life as a shepherd, he soon found employment with a Kendal newspaper (probably *The Westmorland Gazette*) helping to set up printing blocks. His new money enabled him to buy a bicycle and his horizons broadened; it also gave him an interest in cycling which he retained throughout his life. Being ambitious, he secured a job as a junior reporter and spent all his spare time walking and cycling around the Lakes, usually alone. To make sure he spent as much time on the hills as possible he would sleep rough on the fells so as to carry on the next day.

Gradually his walks became more ambitious and he would gladly hike from Kendal to Keswick to explore the northern fells before walking back home again. He boasted that "he could walk the clock around twice without stopping" – once actually managing to walk eighty five miles in twenty six hours. Often shunning paths, he was a true mountaineer who loved nothing better than to follow a contour line around a mountain range for hour after hour. He also became interested in rock climbing and went regularly. He climbed with, and was a friend of, Lehmann J. Oppenheimer (whose *Heart of Lakeland* was one of the early classics about rock climbing in the Wasdale area of the Lakes) and was greatly affected by his death in the Great War. Together with several other friends from Kendal he became an original member of the Fell and Rock Climbing Club in 1906 and was the editor of its journal from 1910-1918 during the difficult war years that saw so many of its members killed on the Western Front. In photographs Palmer is seen usually in tweed jacket and plus fours which were his standard walking attire throughout his life. He was also a prolific camper who used his holidays and breaks as an opportunity to research for his numerous magazine articles and his many books. Claiming to have camped in every county in England, his combination of walking, climbing and living under canvas, made him the ultimate outdoor man.

Although he moved for a time to Liverpool to pursue his journalistic career, he was a Lakes man at heart. He married Annie Iron of the Sommerville K. Shoe family in 1901, and his first book, *Lake Country Rambles* was published in 1902. Between then and his death a steady stream of works followed, and he was at his most active from 1937 onwards. His last book *Byways in Lakeland* was published in 1952. His wife was also a keen walker as well as an amateur botanist and together they formed a formidable team although she never shared his passion for rock climbing. His book *The English Lakes* saw him collaborating with the Grasmere artist Alfred Heaton Cooper and could easily have been chosen for 'The Classic' we are looking at here.

William and Annie had two daughters, Annie and Jean, and were close all their lives. Towards the end of his life he moved to London with his wife so she could be near the specialists she needed as her health failed. She died several months before William who died from Huntington's disease (his two daughters also died from the same illness) which is a neurological disorder and causes problems for the patient in controlling moods, learning new things and in the later stages, even feeding themselves. It was a sad way for a man with such an active mind and free thinking spirit to end his days.

There are so many quotes that can be pulled from his books and so much enjoyment that can be gained. The best thing to do is to buy old copies (they are all out of print now) when you see them and spend time amongst their pages. You will be inspired by what you find.

So, we have two books – *Odd Corners in English Lakeland* and *More Odd Corners in English Lakeland* both of which have photos by Abrahams of Keswick. It can be argued that both are somewhat dated now but any William Palmer book will delight a lover of Lakeland and the outdoors.

Odd Corners first appeared in 1913 and although enjoyed by many, it went out of print and was only available in second hand book outlets. In 1930 the London publisher Skeffington & Son decided to re-publish it and Palmer was asked to bring it up to date and as a result of this he found himself commissioned to write a full series of *Odd Corner* books that included *Odd Corners in North Wales, The Yorkshire Dales and Derbyshire*. His extensive travelling and outdoor lifestyle made him the perfect author to undertake such a project.

Life had changed beyond belief in Lakeland between 1913 and 1930. A world war had altered people's outlook on life – the growing world unrest all around spoke of more trouble ahead and the motor car had replaced the horse drawn carriages that had provided the majority of transport around the region when the first edition came out. We learn that the last horse drawn carriage ran from Windermere to Keswick in 1930 and that regular bus services and more frequent trains were bringing tourists into the area and helping them get around it.

Odd Corners was followed up by *More Odd Corners* in 1937 and together they make a grand collection of facts about the lesser known aspects, areas and people of the Lakes. They were not guidebooks to the main honeypots, but looked more at the secret tracks, the hidden valleys, the ghost stories, the standing stones, the legends and above all, the people. Palmer, like Harry Griffin after him, loved to tell of real people and real lives. Both volumes make fascinating reading and provide eye-opening insights into places you may think you know well but will suddenly discover you don't. William Palmer's style was always readable and interesting and modern day readers will have no problem with it. And once you have got through these two, I guarantee you will seek out the other books from 'The Mystery Man' of Lakeland and who knows, maybe some modern day Skeffington publisher with vision will see the value in re-publishing the majority of his books again and William T Palmer can finally take his place amongst the more familiar of Lakeland's great writers which in truth, is exactly where he deserves to be.

CUMBRIA IN HIS BLOOD – LAKELAND'S NORTH STAR

Next time you are in Keswick, take a drive north up the A591 to the east of Bassenthwaite Lake driving under the slopes of Skiddaw and watch for the buildings of Dancing Gate on your right just before the trees of Thornthwaite Forest. Above it there is a large house that looks like an old school. You will no doubt have noticed it before – this is Dancing Beck, a wonderful property overlooking the north western fells from its elevated position. It was also the last Lakeland home of local author and playwright Graham Sutton. It had indeed been a school and was built in 1850 but was bought by Sutton in the 1950s and converted into a private dwelling. Today it offers bed and breakfast and the present owners are justifiably proud of the building's literary heritage.

Graham Sutton was a man who was Cumbrian through and through and his fictional works chronicling his wonderful Fleming family are classics and a great read. I have chosen his novel *North Star* (published in 1949) out of his many books to be representative of a true 'Lakeland classic' and if you look at location specific literature in any region you will always find that fiction is poorly represented. Most volumes that have stood the test of time are travelogues, travel guides or reminiscences of bygone days and the fact is that most critics would consider a 'classic' for a region such as the Lakes to be tales of true life and happenings and not the figments of the author's imagination. However, storytelling is a true art form in the same vein as painting or poetry writing but unfortunately many authors lack the gift of matching their characters against the real life backgrounds in which they wish to place them in an authentic and convincing way. This is particularly true of 'green fields' locations as opposed to cities or towns and Cumbrian fiction would fall very much into this category. Let's face it, it's difficult enough to capture the reality of what we see on a modern camera, but to try and describe it accurately and use it as the setting for a story is a daunting prospect.

But it didn't appear to be so for Graham Sutton. From his own climbing and walking ventures in the hills he knew the Lakeland fells and surroundings inside out, and when he put pen to paper and described a certain feature you could be sure it would be there and as you read more you would find yourself transported into places you had roamed in yourself and the mind's eye (the aptly named 'skull cinema') takes over and you find yourself actually there in spirit. It takes a skilful and knowledgeable writer to achieve this, but Sutton does it throughout his many books.

North Star is the odd one out in the series of books as it chronicles the adventures of young Ewan Fleming in his ambitions to become a famous actor and break away from the family farm and home at the end of Borrowdale in Seathwaite. Straightaway your mind is transported to this remote farm where you have no doubt parked your car many times before an ascent of Scafell Pike or a trip up Gable. And believe me, Graham Sutton doesn't disappoint his readers once he has captured their minds and placed them where he wants them to be.

From the opening onwards, the background of Upper Borrowdale, Ewan's 'secret valley' of Eskdale and the area around Great Moss are brought alive. Sutton didn't write rip roaring adventure novels, instead he was the master of people studies. His books follow families over generations and piece together how they interact and how their personal agendas affect those around them. He is highly readable and you will find yourself sitting down with his books for far longer than you intended to simply find how what happens to whom and where.

The bulk of *North Star* is based in Borrowdale and around Keswick but parts of it move on to London to follow young Ewan on his quest for greatness. He is different from his predecessors in the Fleming family described in the previous books of the series, (many of whom appear in this one too) being much deeper and far more cunning. In Ewan, Sutton gives us a complicated and over ambitious young man who seems at odds with the beautiful surroundings he lives in. He is manipulative, attractive to women (something he uses shamefully to his advantage) and will stop at nothing to get what he wants. As a hero he is perhaps tainted, but the story that unfolds is fascinating and the end is a brilliant reward. It would spoil it if I let that secret out but you will find it shocking and worth waiting for.

As this is a historical work (Graham Sutton's Fleming novels cover the period from 1745 to 1878) the author also cleverly weaves in real people from the time and brings them alive again in his works. This he does neatly and with skill and uses them to develop his story. In *North Star* we meet William Wordsworth, Hartley Coleridge (who plays quite a central part in matters) the son of Samuel Taylor Coleridge, the iron master John Wilkinson and various famous actors from the period.

North Star is the third in the four books of the Fleming Chronicles, but don't let that put you off. Each is complete in itself and can be read independently of the others. I have to say though, once you get a taste for Sutton and his works you will probably want to read them all.

The first is *Shepherd's Warning* (an eighteenth century story of smuggling and spying in coastal Cumbria), next was *Smoke Across the Fell* (more smuggling that this time takes place inland in the Lakes as opposed to on the coast), then came *North Star* and finally *Fleming of Honister* (more acting and stage sagas and a lot about railways). Together they form a complete history of the fictional Fleming clan and their association with the Lake District and Cumbria as a whole.

Graham Sutton was known as an honest man who disliked deceit and was open in his dealings with others. This transfers to the characters in his books who show great integrity in their day to day lives. The exception to this trait is Ewan in *North Star* who was conceived as a flawed Fleming and the opposite of what Sutton himself stood for.

Ewan is the son of Dirk Fleming a sheep farmer from Seathwaite and one time smuggler. He lives at the valley head with his second wife Jennifer and her father Charles Fanshawe Clute. Add in a little mystery and a background of gypsies, fortune telling and the gift of being able to see the future (as Ewan's true mother was reputed to be able to do – his grandfather had been burnt at the stake in Douglas town square as a wizard) and you start to see just what you are letting yourself in for.

Graham Sutton was a talented writer who also produced short stories (his *Dusk Below Helvellyn* is a chilling tale of the Battle of Dunmail Raise), did radio broadcasts about Cumbria and produced work for *The Fell and Rock Climbing Club* of which he was member. He wrote other works such as the Elizabethan spy story *The Rowan Tree* and the classic *Fell Days* which is a compilation of broadcast talks on Cumbrian hill country he made.

A typical review of Sutton's work gives great credit to his skill of drawing the reader in through his accurate local knowledge. "In his Cumbrian historical novels, Graham Sutton combines breadth of historical perspective, knowledge of the terrain and understanding of the local character, with a captivating skill in story telling which can hold the readers attention."

Sutton was born in Scotby into a family that owned farmlands and a tannery and had done for generations. His father was known as a thorough and meticulous man who was fair in his handlings with people. Young Graham inherited these qualities and was a talented watercolour artist and wood craftsman. He could look at mechanical devices and with little thought dismantle them and put them back together again.

His education began at St Bees School and he went to Queens College Oxford in 1911 after gaining a scholarship. At St Bees he was Head Boy and also *Victor Ludorum* for being the best all round athlete. He was an excellent sportsman with limitless energy and vitality. He played hockey and rugby and turned out for Carlisle Rugby team. At Oxford he took an Honours Degree in English, contributed to *Oxford Poetry* and had a one act play, *Pierrotesque* produced at the Bristol Rep. His father had been a writer too and wrote stories and plays in the unique Cumbrian dialect that was to become such a mark of Graham's later works. A career in acting beckoned, but after a period pursuing it he turned to teaching. He held jobs at Edinburgh Academy and Hammersmith.

All his life he was a 'live wire' full of zest for living and he always insisted in having a house a good walking distance from school or his place of work in order to keep fit for the days on the rocks and fells he loved. During his teaching days he would take regular part in competitive sports and travel extensively at weekends using overnight trains to get to and from his destinations so as to be able to maximise his time on the ground once there.

His first steps into writing came via journalism followed by a bit of broadcasting on country programmes. In his early career he wrote detective stories under the pen name of Anthony Marsden (some of the better known ones being *The Moonstone Mysteries* that were broadcast on radio). In time he left the south to return to the Lakes where he hoped to complete the long held ambition he had to write the fictional history of his Fleming family.

People who have written of Graham Sutton have called him versatile, full of life and fun, energetic to the point of overflowing, zestful and thorough. He was a people person and that shows in this books. Other people's lives fascinated him and he liked to learn from experts on any subject.

Perhaps the words on his gravestone, which you will find in All Saints Churchyard at Scotby, sum him up best of all: "He loved Cumbria and his fellow man".

THE FIRST RECORDED FELL WALKER

'In Xanadu did Kubla Khan
A stately pleasure dome decree:

Where Alph, the sacred river, ran
Through caverns measureless to man
Down to a sunless sea.'

Kubla Khan is, next to *The Rime of the Ancient Mariner*, the best
known of the poems of the Romantic poet Samuel Taylor Coleridge
and one that a lot of us had to study in school. Although we may be
aware that the text was conceived by Coleridge in an opium induced
dream, if you are a Lakeland lover it will interest you to know that
the poet envisaged his fictional location for the pleasure dome to be
in the depths of Dungeon Gill in Great Langdale.

That's the wonderful thing about Coleridge. Many of his works
were inspired by his love affair with the Lakes and his letters are full
of places we know and visit regularly. And he was probably the first
climber and fell walker in the lakes to go into print on a regular basis.

This chapter is a little bit unusual in that the book we are going
to look at was not by the person we are concerned with here. *The
Collected Letters of Samuel Taylor Coleridge* is a six volume collection
that was compiled by the New York research professor Earl Leslie
Griggs (1899-1975) over a forty year period between the 1930s
and 1972. From early in his career he set out to concentrate on
the English Romantic poets and in particular, the works and life
of Coleridge. His determination resulted in him producing sixteen
books and over forty papers on the Romantic poet era.

The Collected Letters is an almost complete journey through the
poet's adult life, but I have selected volume two which covers the years
1801-1806 to look at and recommend as a real 'Lakeland classic'.

This period covers a very settled time in the often troubled
life of this gifted man, a time when he followed his great friends
William Wordsworth and Robert Southey to the Lake District
and settled there, roaming the fells and finding the contentment
that often eluded him throughout his years. Coleridge was many

things – sickly, often addicted to opium (taken to relieve his various ailments), fallible in many ways, trapped in a loveless marriage and in love with another woman he could never be with. He was often inconsistent and left lots of things and pieces of work unfinished, but for the purpose of our feature today we will concentrate on Coleridge the lover of Lakeland and the first fell walker and climber who put pen to paper and recorded his routes in print.

We have much to thank him for outside of his poetry. *Lyrical Ballads*, which he co-wrote with William Wordsworth while still a young man, has long been considered a classic of English literature. I have to admit that I never really got to grips with it during my school days but found it fascinating as I got older. You will have no such problems with Coleridge's letter writing. He was prolific with his pen and volume two of those that E. L. Griggs so skilfully put together for us is a delight to read if you have even just a passing interest in the Lake District. Here we get a picture of the Lakes of the eighteenth and early nineteenth centuries as seen through the eyes of one who looked deeply into all he saw. Many famous people appear as recipients of his letters: the Wordsworths, Robert Southey (whom he wrote to and stayed with often), Humphrey Davey, Charles Lamb, his often ailing wife who he seemed to be apart from so often and of course, the woman he loved but could never marry, Sara Hutchinson.

It's a remarkable collection penned mostly from locations you will be familiar with. It shows the day to day life of a man who loved his work and the surroundings he found himself in. The letters show his hopes and dreams, his fears and the daily thoughts that occupied the people of the day. *Collected Letters* is highly sought after and would cost quite a bit at a rare book shop or book fair. Libraries can track down copies with a little persuasion and it's always worth keeping an eye open in junk shops, car boot sales and the like – you never know;

my own book collection (which is currently outgrowing the room I have it in) has many rare volumes bought cheaply in this fashion.

And the very best thing you will find in Coleridge's letters also appears in volume two, this being the first recorded descent of Broad Stand between Scafell and Scafell Pike. It is still a fairly risky proposition today and often the scene of accidents. For its time, the descent was an epic adventure and a feat of great courage for a man with no rope and no knowledge of the terrain that lay below him. However, Coleridge was a ground breaking walker and scrambler who appeared to have little fear in mountain country.

It may interest you to know that in September 1800 he made the first recorded round of the classic fells that surround Coledale. Today when we march merrily from Grisedale Pike to either Barrow or Causey Pike (depending on our preference) we are following in his footsteps. He undertook the daring venture on a night time moonlit trip along the Helvellyn Ridge, over the Dodds, to visit his good friends the Wordsworths at Grasmere. To many, night time hill walking today is still a secret world where they dare not venture even with head torch and GPS. Imagine how much of a feat it was on a night in 1800 armed only with only a 'fellpole' (the Lakeland equivalent of the Swiss alpenstock and a dangerous implement that was easy to trip over).

Coleridge liked to walk alone. He enjoyed the physical pleasure of pushing himself in the hills but needed the more spiritual connection that being by himself gave him. "I must be alone if my imagination and heart are to be enriched" he tells us. He got lost in mist on Carrock Fell in 1800 and stumbled into the cottage of an old woman who gave him food – he also spent much time exploring Bowscale Fell and Bannerdale Crags from both Mungrisdale and Keswick. But above all, his time on Broad Stand is what grips the imagination.

Turn back the time to 5 August 1802. After climbing Scafell by the Green How route he spent time writing (another letter in fact) on the summit. Looking for a way down he scouted around the rim of Scafell Crag and saw Mickledore (like many have since) enticingly close below. Sensibly throwing his 'fellpole' down ahead of him he began his descent. As you read his letter to his love Sara Hutchinson you will find yourself reliving his adventure step for step. Even today, with plenty of knowledge of what lies ahead, it would be a scary proposition.

For its time it was ground breaking and it is little wonder that the poet found himself with "shaky legs" and "heat bumps" on reaching the bottom safely. It has been speculated since that what Coleridge actually finished down was the neighbouring Mickledore Chimney and that the Broad Stand we see today at Mickledore is the result of the over zealous use of explosives. Regardless it was a great achievement and we are lucky that it was done by a man whose gift of putting his experiences into written words was so adept.

As with a lot of Coleridge works the letter was a little incomplete. He returned to Keswick on 10 August and wrote to Sara saying he had yet to finish it properly. As far as we are aware he never did. He wrote his initial account from a farmhouse in Eskdale and for this one letter alone the second volume of *Collected Letters* is worth reading. But there is so much more here for Lakeland lovers. Search out a copy and go back in time to those heady days when the fells and the way up them were still a great mystery to all who lived near them.

Coleridge's life is well documented but perhaps a brief overview is needed here to complete this piece. He was an interesting man but had a degree of self-loathing that could often border on manic depression. He was born in Ottery St Mary in Devon on 21 October 1772 and died in Highgate, London on 25 July 1834. The son of a clergyman he was known as a child who daydreamed a lot. After his father's death he was sent away to Christ's Hospital School in London. Being talented he finally arrived at Cambridge University where he met the radical Robert Southey who would remain a lifelong friend. In 1795 he married Sara Fricker the sister of Southey's fiancée Edith who he didn't really love but wed only because of the social constraints of the time. He grew to detest his wife and finally divorced her. He fell in love with a woman named Sara Hutchinson who did not reciprocate his passion causing him great distress and heartache. His first real work, *Poems on Various Subjects* was published in 1796 the year after he met William and Dorothy Wordsworth who became good friends. He began to take laudanum (an opium derivative) in 1796, initially for pain relief; it has to be said that there was no stigma attached to the use of opium at the time but little was understood about the harmful and addictive effects it could have. In the autumn of 1798 he visited Germany with Wordsworth, soon going his own way and on returning to England in 1800, he settled in Keswick with his family. After initial good times his health deteriorated along with his marriage and mental state.

Between 1804 and 1810 he took work in Malta and travelled extensively in Italy. His opium addiction was getting out of control and he fell out with Wordsworth in 1810 two years after divorcing his wife. Lecturing in London and Bristol between 1810 and 1820 led him to live in the capital, eventually in the home of the physician James Gillman, and it was here he completed his long term autobiographical project *Biographia Literaria* in 1815. He died from a lung disorder and heart failure caused by opium abuse.

A sad end to a talented life. Perhaps for us he is best remembered as the happy young man striding over the Lakeland fells and making his dashing and daring descent of the rocks of Broad Stand just over two hundred years ago.

THE MAN WHO INSPIRED WAINWRIGHT

The next time you drive from Windermere to Bowness watch out for the Baddeley memorial clock at the junction of New Road and Lake Road. You will have probably passed it many times before but not really taken much notice of it except to note, in passing, that it seems to have always been there and looks old.

It was erected in 1907 in memory of the prolific guidebook writer Mountford John Byrde Baddeley who had died a year earlier and whose contribution to classic Lakeland literature is underrated and often little known.

And yet his comprehensive book *Baddeley's Guide to the English Lake District*, which was originally published as the first in his *Thorough GuideBook* series under the title, *Thorough Guide to the English Lake District* in 1880, went on to undergo twenty one reprints. The final one was in 1956 and that's a track record most guidebook writers can only dream of.

Seventy six years in print meant a lot of changes and obviously revisions took place as reprints were published but the basic format and content of this wonderful, and now rare guidebook, remained much the same as the original. True the subject matter, the Lake District, changed beyond belief in those years, but the foundation of the book, the fells, the lakes and the paths would always remain a constant. The copies you are most likely to come across today (and that still sell on e-bay if you fancy looking) are in the Ward Lock & Co *Illustrated Red Guide* series. Ebenezer Ward and George Lock originally set up Ward Lock in 1854 on Fleet Street in London to offer a range of books at reasonable prices aimed at the ever growing market of readers whose general interests included cooking, gardening and cheap throwaway novels. The company produced its classic *Red Guides* to most areas of the United Kingdom in the 1920s and 30s and Baddeley's *Thorough Guide* was incorporated into it with the 'Thorough' being dropped at this time. I was fascinated to learn when researching this author that there is a large collecting and trading club that currently seeks out these *Red Guides*, and that some of the rarer ones can fetch a lot of money.

Before Ward Lock acquired Baddeley's series, it was published by Dulau & Co and later by Thomas Nelson & Sons. And it really was what the original title claimed – a thorough guide to Lakeland that covered everything a prospective visitor could wish for.

A long way south of the Lakes, in Devon, the classic guidebook to that area is of a similar age and called *Crossings Guide to Dartmoor*, and all who seek to explore the area are urged to use a copy of it as a basis for their explorations despite its age. And so it is with M.J.B. Baddeley's guide. It is very thorough and although a lot of what it contains may be dated, the general information, especially the three Bartholomew drawn pull out panoramas of summit views, is very useful. There are also a lot of pull out maps which, depending on the condition of the copy you get, may or may not be there and are of less use and certainly show their age.

But surely a true 'classic' work doesn't still have to be totally relevant to its subject matter and a lot of its status may be well due to the historic value of the written pages? As with Wordsworth's classic *Guide to the Lakes*, old accounts of how things were are often as interesting as up to date monologues that tell of the latest paths up Latrigg (for instance).

Another thing that makes Baddeley of interest is that our old friend and guru of all Lakeland guidebook writers, Alfred Wainwright, knew his work and used it. Take the pull-out panorama from Helvellyn summit as produced by Baddeley (done in pen and ink with blue for sky and lake) and you can see instantly where Wainwright got his ideas from. He only differed in the fact that he wanted to be very fell specific whereas Baddeley had only covered in detail what he considered to be the twenty best known Lakeland Fells and the rest of his book was of more general content covering walks, transport, towns, geology, flora and fauna and the like.

The other main difference between Baddeley and Wainwright was that Baddeley chose a more text based approach to his guide whereas Wainwright illustrated heavily with drawings. This was probably because around the time he wrote it, the likes of the Abraham Brothers were producing quality photographic guides for walkers and climbers and his intention was to produce something a little more unique.

This is exactly what he did and it has to be said that if we are looking here, and we are, at the man who was one of the inspirations for Wainwright then we have to sit up and take note.

So if you decide to track a copy of *Guide to the English Lake District* down, what do you get for your money? First a note of caution. Be wary of internet auction sites where the collectors may push the price up. I picked up my copy of Baddeley's guide through the internet site Abe Books (www.abebooks.com) and it cost me £6.00 including postage and packing. Libraries seem to struggle with locating it but put in a bit of effort and get yourself a copy you can keep. It's a great little volume, pocket sized and three hundred pages plus in length and although you probably won't carry it around with you to treat as an 'up to date' guide, its historic relevance and the wealth of information it contains will give this book a treasured place on your bookshelf.

The later reprints moved with the times to include details of such 'modern' things as locations of phone boxes in public places and I have often thought it would be a fun exercise to take the list of these and see if they still exist at the points indicated. This is by the by and a little bit of a fun distraction, but the real treasure of Baddeley's guide is the blanket coverage it gives to an area we know and love. All aspects of the Lakes are looked at and although the twenty maps and plans may be a little obsolete (apart from the summit views) they are good fun to look at. When was the last time you surveyed a road map of Cumbria with no M6 on it?

This comprehensive guidebook starts with a look at Lakeland generally – history, weather, geology, natural history, heights of passes, mountains and waterfalls and carries on to look carefully at all sport undertaken in the region from climbing and fell walking to golf and yachting.

All the principal centres are covered with walk descriptions from each, motoring and cycling are given a section and various approaches to the district are discussed. I particularly enjoyed the 'days on the fells' chapter and 'descents from the fells', both of which are a delightful look at routes that will be familiar to us today in most cases.

As a read it's done in a factual way rather than a chatty style, but Baddeley was a studious man who took things very seriously.

Mountford John Byrde Baddeley was born on 6 March 1843 in Uttoxeter, Staffordshire and died of pneumonia on 19 November 1906 at 2 Lake View Villas, Bowness. An intelligent student, he obtained a classical scholarship at Clare College, Cambridge and eventually graduated BA with a second class in the classical Tripos in 1868. From 1869 onwards he earned a living as a teacher and on retirement moved to 'The Hollies' in Windermere before moving to his final home at Lake View Villas, Bowness. He knew the Lake District well and was keenly interested in local affairs and he became the Chairman of the Bowness Local Board until it was dissolved in 1894. He was an original champion of footpath preservation and an early promoter of outdoor tourism in the area.

Baddeley's achievements were many and included setting up parties to regularly visit the passes and report on their condition and it was on his insistence that signs were first placed on mountain paths. The new road from Skelwith Bridge to Langdale and the road along the western side of Thirlmere were tributes to his tireless campaigning. He was an enthusiastic walker and nature lover who enjoyed the outdoors up until his death aged sixty three. The later years of his life were taken up walking throughout the United Kingdom and compiling his series of *Thorough Guides* to various areas, the Lake District one being the first. It was his most popular guidebook and although the series extended to fifteen titles, he never surpassed his Lakeland volume.

He was a practical writer, accurate and concise in the smallest of details whose real gift was in the colourful descriptions he painted of the natural scene. He swayed towards the walker in his works but was not an advocator of dangerous pursuits at all. He married Millicent Satterthwaite a local Windermere lady in 1891 and was buried at Bowness after his death.

Mountford Baddeley was a true son of Lakeland who deserves to be better known by readers of Lakeland literature. Go and take a look at his memorial clock again, get hold of a copy of his book and let me leave you with some of his introductory words from the guide which we can all identify with: "There is probably no beauty spot in the world which can equal English Lakeland".

Praise indeed from a man who had seen a lot of them.

A CHAMPION OF CONSERVATION

I have three copies of Henry Herbert Symonds' wonderful book *Walking in The Lake District* in my library. It's not surprising really as, after its initial publication in April 1933, this classic Lakeland work was re-published no fewer than five more times before 1947 and was re-printed again as late as 1962 by Chambers, which gives you some indication of its enormous popularity.

Interestingly, the 1962 edition was a little more than just another reprint being an updated and new edition. Susan Johnson is the granddaughter of H.H. Symonds and lives in Cockermouth and she told me that this later version had all the routes checked and updated where necessary by the author's daughter who was her mother.

Originally described by one reviewer as "a delightful book – he (Symonds) knows the hills in the right way". *Walking in the Lake District* is a wonderful read and I only hope that someone will be kind enough to write such a glowing testament to me one day.

Knowing our Lakeland hills in the correct manner is a true tribute to this very interesting man who lived a fascinating life and was influential in many of the areas of outdoor Cumbrian life we take for granted today.

Walking in the Lake District was his one and only major book (there was a smaller one concerning the forestry in Lakeland about which more later) but what a tribute it became to its author and what a way to be remembered. "There can be no safer nor more genial companion for the fell wanderer" wrote *The Yorkshire Post* of this book, and no lesser authority than the *Times Literary Supplement* waxed lyrical about the virtues of this lovely volume claiming its author "can tell you every gate, wire fence and footbridge in a hundred walks from Ravenglass to Mungrisedale, from Shap to Loweswater".

And that really sums up the appeal of H.H. Symonds as most people refer to him. He had an in-depth and intimate knowledge of the terrain and landscape of the lakes and fells, he was passionate about spending time amongst them and was obsessed with preserving them for later generations. And yet he was a quiet man, little known to the general public and one is left with the abiding wish that he might have put pen to paper more often and transferred some of that encyclopaedic knowledge he had stored in his head onto paper.

He was a talented writer who used a chatty style that relaxed his readers and indulged them in a 'mind tour' of a landscape they loved. He wrote in a time before Mardale was flooded, before the trains had their branchlines cut back and still ran far into the region, and well before the Lakes had achieved National Park status; and yet this forward thinking and clever writer could see all these changes on the horizon and his book is not just a guidebook to what could be seen at the time but was also almost a 'literary time capsule' to a world that would be changed forever by a world war and rapid advances in communication and technology.

Take a copy of *Walking in the Lake District* somewhere quiet and allow yourself to be transported back to the world of Lakeland pre-1939 when roads were quieter and much, much narrower and the world was a simpler place to live. The book has several black and white photographs that will be of interest to the reader and the one I particularly like is the shot of the old road into Great Langdale which looks little more than a cart track as it winds along the valley. But it is for the prose that you will enjoy this book the most. Symonds literally takes you by the hand and walks you into the Lakes from the west beginning your tour at Shap Station – see what I mean about indulging in nostalgia as you read! This is the old Shap Station on the West Coast Mainline which was closed in 1968.

And from there you are swept into the valleys and fells of the Lakes and shown many hidden corners you may have forgotten or never known. Ancient tracks are explored, valleys ferreted around and the tops visited. This is more than just a description of a walk around the Lakes, this is one man's knowledge of a landscape he loves deeply being committed to paper and written in such a way as to make easy reading and provoke instant memories.

You will enjoy Symonds' style and the pictures he paints of the landscape, and most of all you will revel in the in-depth knowledge he imparts to his reader. Nothing escapes his eye and interest and you feel as though there is no corner of a hidden dale head or summit cairn he has not visited or doesn't have a view on. Reading Symonds reminds me very much of browsing through Wainwright's guides but without the drawings. Both men had an unbelievable knowledge of the region and knew how to pass that on to others. One feels they would have been kindred spirits had they known each other.

In his introduction to *Walking in the Lake District*, Symonds states simply that "no man who uses a map need grow old" and one is instantly reminded of Wainwright and his descriptions of maps as "old friends" that could be brought out and past days relived and retraced with a finger. Was Symonds referring to something like this or perhaps to the way maps revitalise old legs once they are laid out and yet one more hill day is planned, or was it both?

In *Walking in the Lake District* the region is completely covered by chapters on all major areas and, as well as that, itineraries are included for walking tours with other chapters written covering such things as 'The National Trust in the Lakes' which the author was very interested in. There is a section on walking hints and a highly readable chapter on 'The Making of the Mountains' which covers the evolution of mountain landscape and natural history. All in all a very complete book to Lakeland which was way ahead of its time if a little out of date now.

Symonds was born in 1885 and died in 1958, and although he worked as teacher for much of his life, he was also a vicar. He is, as far as I can tell, one of the only modern day writers to have had a summit named after him, that being Symonds Knott on Scafell. Symonds studied Classics at Oxford and went on to teach at Rugby School as Head of Classics, but later became headmaster of the Liverpool Institute from 1924-1935.

During this period of his life he became a formidable figure in the emerging social movement for access to the countryside and for the protection of our open spaces and wild land. An ever increasing portion of his free time was given over to the campaign for the establishment of National Parks in our country and his overriding passion for the Lake District and the preservation of it for future generations came to the forefront.

During the1930s, tree planting in valleys and on high ground became a hot topic, and a particularly burning issue amongst the new breed of conservationists was the afforestation of Ennerdale by the Forestry Commission which was bitterly opposed by Symonds and all who walked the Lakeland fells. He produced another small book which was never as well known as *Walking in the Lake District*, called *Afforestation in the Lake District*. He was a leading light in the campaign against the Forestry Commission's plans and when a deal was struck to limit ground loss, he was very satisfied with what he had achieved.

He was also a founder member of the Friends of the Lake District (formed in 1934) and was a pioneer who promoted the growth of Youth Hostelling not only in Lakeland, but nationwide.

H.H. Symonds died on 28 December 1958 and it is fitting that a mountain bears his name. He was a gifted author who paid great care to detail as he wrote and, with his accessible style, passed on his passion for the wild places of the Lakes.

People of this sort are always missed and more of the same calibre are always needed. It's nice to think that at least one of them, Lakeland's very own champion of conservation can be remembered via the fitting tribute of a book he wrote from the heart.

A Backwoodsman without a Beard

In 1961 John Wyatt got the job as the first warden of the infant Lake District National Park. It was a post he beat five hundred other applicants to, and it was a job he had set his heart on getting. Lady

Lowther, part of the interviewing panel, later told him that she had voted for him because all the other potential employees for this sought after position had beards and he didn't.

It's a lovely sentiment and a nice story that sums up author, naturalist and Lake District lover John Wyatt perfectly. He was different; he wasn't what people expected him to be and he had a clear vision from a young man of what he wanted to do.

His best known book, *The Shining Levels*, was first published in 1973 and must be one of the most atmospheric works on Lakeland ever written. Many books on the district tell of the mountains and the lakes and epic trips over and across them. There are very few that concentrate on the forests and woodlands of the area; on the animals and the trees and flowers. *The Shining Levels* is unique and provides a wonderful nostalgic read for Lake District lovers far and wide whether native to the region or estranged from it and wanting something to remind them of what they are missing.

Sadly, John Wyatt died on 19 March 2006 at the age of 81, but what a legacy he left behind him. Here was a true son of the Lakes despite the fact he was born in Ashton under Lyne many miles south of the county he came to adopt and love so much.

Apart from *The Shining Levels* he was the author of over ten other books on Lakeland including *Reflections on the Lakes* and *The Bliss of Solitude* as well as a series of guides under the pseudonym John Parker. These guides under the heading *Lake District Walks for Motorists*, and divided into three areas of the Lakes, are hard to find nowadays but are readable and interesting if you manage to track one down. Why did he adopt a pseudonym for these titles? Well, as an employee of the National Park his then boss would not allow him to turn his experiences into profit from other means. So he wrote under a different name and the books sold well.

John Wyatt was born on 16 January 1925 and must be admired by all country lovers as not only a great writer but a man who followed his dream and lived his life on his own terms. How often do we plan to 'drop out' and get away from the rat race, to live close to nature away from the stress and hustle and bustle of modern times? It is a dream that man has had for ages past and will no doubt have for centuries to come.

John Wyatt was a man who achieved this and prospered. *The Shining Levels* is subtitled *The Story of a Man Who Went Back to Nature* and this is exactly what it is, a warm and extremely well written story by someone who knew his environment and could convey his feelings for what he did to other like-minded folk through the medium of words.

Great Tower Scout Camp and the surrounding woodland where much of the action in *The Shining Levels* takes place is still a regular part of Lakeland life. The camp is situated close to the east shore of Windermere between Newby Bridge and Bowness and still provides adventure holidays for young people in its 250 acres of woodland and fell. Situated on the pretty Birks Road between the A592 and the A5074 it must have been a haven of solitude and peace in the days when John Wyatt knew and loved it. His descriptions of the area are dramatic, his love for it obvious to anyone who reads his books.

Wyatt was a self taught writer and *The Shining Levels* was his first proper book. He visited the Lakes for the first time as part of a Scout group on a holiday at Great Tower and knew that was where he belonged. A little like Alfred Wainwright standing on the summit of Orrest Head and knowing his future lay in all he saw around him, John Wyatt never quite got over that first encounter with Lakeland. After leaving school he worked for *The Daily Telegraph* but the call of the Lakes was strong and he soon found himself back at Great Tower as a warden and a forestry worker. During the Second World War he left to do his national service in the Navy and after demob took up the position of sub-postmaster in the town of his birth. But the Lakes – the shining levels of his book – were never far from his thoughts and it was not long after that he returned again, this time to stay. When he became the National Park's first warden his responsibility was for the whole of the Lake District, but two years later another warden joined and the region was split into two with John taking responsibility for the southern Lake District. After 1974 wardens became known as rangers and he rose to become the Chief Ranger and in 1986 received an MBE for services to the area. In retirement John Wyatt continued to write and several books followed, his final one being *The Lake District and its County* in 2004.

John will be remembered for many things from his work and commitment to Lakeland and for his colourful and beautiful writing but it will be *The Shining Levels* that will be his most enduring memorial. It is not a particularly long book but contains warmth, humour, information and an insight into a life many of us can only imagine we may one day stumble upon.

Wyatt's shining levels – the lakes of the region as viewed from the heights – provide the background to this marvellous work but it is the author's love of the forests, of nature, of the flora and fauna he sees all around him that will endear this book to modern day readers. It's nice to think that this work is recent enough to tell of times still remembered by many older people; and what a place of peace and tranquillity the Lakes must have been then with fewer cars and no motorway to whisk visitors up there in a couple of hours. It would have seemed the ideal place to 'run away' to for a young man of John Wyatt's calibre. And he found there all he could have hoped for.

The Shining Levels tells of life in the Great Wood where the author lived in a small cabin with no running water and no electricity. An existence that seems unbelievable to most of us today and yet when described in his atmospheric style it sounds idyllic and a state to yearn for. We read of the life of the woods, of the life of a forester and of the devastating effect fire could have on woodland. And just when we believe that a remote life of this sort is what we want the author takes us on another step and retires deep into the heart of the wood to live off the land in a shelter he made himself under a fallen tree root. This is backwoodsmanship in all its glory and it sounds magnificent.

Most of all *The Shining Levels* tells us of the friendship between the author and an abandoned roe deer fawn he calls Buck. It is an enchanting story that recalls a relationship that most people would have thought impossible, but in reality developed as naturally as John Wyatt's own progression to the way of life he long desired.

"Going back to nature was never more vividly described" was one review I read and to that you could easily add "and never made to sound more desirable".

I think *The Shining Levels* is the perfect reading for a winter's night when the mind can be left to wander and dreams can be formed for the following year. "Summer is reluctant to leave the Lake District, it says farewell so many times", the author tells us in his warm way. We who love the Lake District know how it feels. My only fear is that of the many who will now read this wonderful book, a lot will become discontent with their lot in life and plan to escape like John Wyatt did.

It's not as simple now as it was then, but dreaming is one of life's great and cheapest luxuries. Writers who inspire readers to dream thus are always needed.

Fittingly, John Wyatt received a private burial in his beloved Lakeland woods and a yew tree was planted over his grave.

PAINTING LAKELAND PANORAMAS – THE HEATON COOPER PHENOMENA

I would like to finish this chapter, with a look at a Lakeland painter, or if you like, a family line of painters. They produced and illustrated books as well and many of them (the books that is – but the paintings more so) have become much sought after collectors items.

I am sure you will already have an idea of who I am talking about here. If we think of the main art forms that Lakeland literature has invoked down the years we quickly realise that there were three distinct masters covering each sector individually. W.A. Poucher was the supreme photographer, Alfred Wainwright the master sketcher and guidebook compiler; and as for painting in watercolours there are none to match Grasmere's William Heaton Cooper (and his father Alfred before him).

The name of William Heaton Cooper is almost synonymous with warm paintings of sunlit fells and glowing mountain panoramas. His work is still much sort after today with pieces sold for high prices at auction houses such as Christies. And from a local landscape painter he became a worldwide phenomenon – the late Harry Griffin recalls seeing Heaton Cooper prints as far afield as New Zealand and British Columbia. Although sought after by collectors they are also much in demand by ordinary mortals such as you and I who find they stir within us a longing for the places of Lakeland we know and love.

There are two books I would recommend right at the start for all who have an interest in the Coopers' art; the first is William's wonderful autobiography *Mountain Painter* which is alive with his paintings and then there is the biography of his father, Alfred, simply called *Alfred Heaton Cooper – Painter of Landscapes* by Jane Renouf. The former is an older volume (1984) and the latter more recent and readily available at the Heaton Cooper studio museum shop in Grasmere.

With copies of these in hand, the interested can become absorbed in the lives of two of Lakeland's greatest landscape painters.

But it is the work of William we will look at here today and in particular his 1960 classic *The Tarns of Lakeland*. There were other books too of course, his *Hills of Lakeland* must share similar 'classic' status, and both William and his father Alfred had work published in many books by other authors.

As a member of the Fell and Rock Climbing Club (and later an honorary member) William's drawings of routes up Lakeland Crags were both exceedingly accurate and often used in climbing guides to the region. In his early years he was an active rock climber who took part in a number of first ascents and the knowledge of the topography of Lakeland rock he gained in this period made his paintings and drawings extremely accurate and true to life.

The Tarns of Lakeland has been on my bookshelf for many years and is a firm favourite, brought down frequently after a trip into the Lakeland hills or often to just sit with on a rainy afternoon in the conservatory and dream of the better days amongst the fells. It is a book that is warm both in colour and to read. William Heaton Cooper had the gift of being able to transmit the wonder and awe of all he saw, along with the peace he felt, into print and into his paintings and drawings. *The Tarns of Lakeland* is a wonderful book rich in detail and full of interest to all Lakeland lovers. It is perhaps not a complete list of Lakeland tarns in the style of John and Anne Nuttall's two volume *Tarns of Lakeland*, but is nevertheless an in-depth look at most of the famous (and some not so well known) tarns that the author knew and loved.

In defining his selection Cooper wrote "I have allowed myself to be free to include anything that had the feel and character of a tarn and in which I had found delight" which is as good a selection process as any. He also added that size, elevation above a main valley and whether they were already called a tarn affected selection but, most of all, "as I am a painter, what the place looks like and what one sees from it".

That is a definition that will do for me. In many ways this was a bold book for its time. Nowadays we are used to seeing volumes on all sorts of diverse Lakeland subjects, but almost fifty years ago the books that sold well looked at the tops and the routes to them. This was a period when Wainwright was enjoying great success and the public's interest was directed to the high places. A book about the tarns would have been deemed unusual and yet with the fame of Heaton Cooper's paintings it was well received and soon became popular.

The book's foreword is a lovely reminiscence by Sir John Hunt (of Everest fame) of a climbing adventure shared with William in the final days of peace before the outbreak of the Second World War and it sets the tone and style of what is to follow perfectly. In his introduction Heaton Cooper tells of how he came to write such a book after being asked two leading questions, firstly about his favourite sort of country and secondly on how many tarns there were in the Lakes.

As he explains, one thing led to another and the outcome was the wonderfully balanced *Tarns of Lakeland* which is well researched, full of accurate facts and off-set with a warm text and Cooper's wonderful paintings and sketches. Very soon after starting the project he realised the enormity of the task he had allowed himself to undertake as there was little else at the time in print on the subject.

This only inspired him further and what transpired can be classed as a remarkable piece of literature for those interested from a scientific stance, those who are merely curious and those of us whose first love is the wild country of Lakeland's fell land. Each tarn dealt with is given a maximum depth (carefully researched), an altitude, surface area and grid reference and there is also text on the surrounding area, the tarn itself and any relevant background or interesting tales the author may have.

"This book will only fulfil its purpose", he wrote, "if it inspires the reader enough to get out a map, put on his boots and go and find each tarn for himself". This it does well, but it also gives us a wonderful 'coffee table' book to lose ourselves in when we have need of escape from day to day pressures.

I'll let you read the book for yourself but amongst the interesting facts you will find in its pages is that Blea Water (High Street range) has a maximum depth of 207 feet and that only two lakes in Cumbria, Windermere and Wastwater are deeper than this tarn.

The Heaton Cooper dynasty is now into its fourth generation at the Grasmere Studios today with William's son, Julian exhibiting oil paintings of the world's mountain regions and his daughter Otalla showing pottery.

So what do we know of the man himself? William Heaton Cooper was the third child of the artist Alfred Heaton Cooper and his Norwegian wife Mathilde. Alfred (1864-1929) was one of the most famous Lake District artists of his time and his style was distinct and different from William's. He made his living purely from his painting and moved several times before settling in the Lakes where the thriving tourist industry promised a regular outlet for his work. William was born in Consiton on 6 October 1903 and at an early age he decided he wanted to paint as his father did. He studied art at the Royal Academy School in London and progressed to hold many exhibitions in the capital and surrounding areas. He was elected a member of the Royal Institute of Painters in water colours in 1953 and for over a decade was President of the Lakes Artists' Society.

When his father died William returned to the Lakes from the south of England where he had been living in an experimental commune. Alfred had built a studio in Ambleside and William found he now had to run it to enable him to look after his mother and younger sister. The period that followed was an unsettled time in his life and it was during this time that he discovered his deep-rooted Christian beliefs and became an active member of the Reverend Frank Buchman's Oxford Group which was later renamed as Moral Rearmament and still exists today as Initiatives of Change. This was an informal international network of people of all faiths (Mary Whitehouse was on of its famous members) who based their Christian beliefs on the 'Four Absolutes' – absolute honesty, absolute purity, absolute unselfishness and absolute love. William always believed that only his religion had made his life truly worthwhile. Deciding to hand over control of his whole life to God he referred afterwards to this moment as his 'release'.

As his painting improved his reputation grew and he was soon considered even greater than his father. Before long the decision was made to move the business to Grasmere and work began on a home and studio there in 1938. In this same year he met the sculptress Ophelia Gordon Bell whom he married in 1940.

William was a good businessman and identifying a fault in the way the family's business ran he set about righting it. Like his father before him he had produced a constant stream of 'original' paintings to keep money coming in. After the Second World War (in which he served as a camouflage Officer) the idea of selling 'reproductions' occurred to him. This was a new concept at the time and took courage to follow through but his instincts proved right and thousands of prints were sold over the years that followed.

He has been described as one of the best selling artists of all time. He loved to paint in the enchanting light of evening or dawn and often tramped the fells for miles to get to suitable spots for this time of the day. Being first and foremost an outdoor painter, most of his work was done 'on the spot' out amongst the hills and later completed in his studio. With his wife he had four children and they lived and were well known in the Grasmere area.

He stayed true to his religion which gave him particular comfort after the early death of his wife in 1975. William continued to paint out on the fells until into his early eighties and Harry Griffin (who wrote his obituary for *The Independent*) recalls meeting him around this time on an autumn day under Ill Crag painting the rock face as carefully as ever. Griffin recalls too how it was William, in the mid 1950s, who had encouraged him to write his first books (destined to become classics in their own right too).

William Heaton Cooper died at the age of ninety one in 1995 but his legacy, like his father's before him, lives on not only in the modern day Grasmere studio but in the vast output of work he left behind and which we still come across today in unexpected places and as we turn the pages of unfamiliar books.

VI.

Epilogue

On the bookshelf in my study I have an old book from 1946 which bears the title *The Lure of Lakeland* – a similar one to this volume, but this is purely coincidental. What brings me to mention this small work (it is only sixty two pages long) is the fact that out of my own very large collection of books on the world's mountainous regions, and especially on the Lakes, I often take this one down to the exception of all others. The author is unknown to me, one E.D. Tinne, but in the few pages he wrote he described a landscape he loved and cherished and his passion for the region shone through in his words and his watercolour paintings. He (I am assuming 'he' was a 'he'!) was a true son of the Lakes and I hope you have seen through these pages that have gone that I am too.

I hope also that my book will be taken down often from your bookshelf to be re-read and enjoyed over and again. And not just on those wild winter's nights when you open your reading matter by the fire and dream of the longer days now vanished for some time.

I sincerely hope you will be inspired by what has gone before to go out and try some of the ideas for yourself. I appreciate they may be a little unorthodox but if they give another aspect to your fell days, I will have achieved much.

I would like to think that my own stories of friends past and present and days spent up high and down low in all sorts of weather and circumstances, may start you reminiscing about your own hill time. Life is very short and the days when our health allows us to enjoy simple and inexpensive pleasures such as climbing to summits can, for many, be even shorter.

Let's make the most of every opportunity we get offered and milk it for all the pleasure it can give us. And let us too be tolerant of the others who share our hill space. Their way of enjoying their days may seem strange to you but it is merely different and each really should be left to his own.

So many other things will vie for our time – families, jobs, homes and so on – but in a world seemingly out of control and fuelled by competitive urge, one-upmanship, greed and stress it is surely refreshing to have a pastime that is so obviously different. Let's all work to keep it that way.

There is an almost Nirvana state that lovers of the outdoors can achieve when they meditate on winter nights by a roaring fire. Past days are re-lived in the 'skull cinema' of the mind and plans for future days and reunions with friends are fulfilled and put into a time scale. And somewhere in the middle of the two is a region of calm and perfect content.

I hope this book helps you to get there.

INDEX